JM: For Andy, always
AS: For Mom & Dad

Published in the United States by Potter Craft, an imprint of the
Crown Publishing Group, a division of Random House, Inc., New York.
www.clarksonpotter.com
www.pottercraft.com

POTTER CRAFT and CLARKSON N. POTTER are trademarks, and
POTTER and colophon are registered trademarks of Random House, Inc.

Library of Congress Cataloging-in-Publication Data is available.

ISBN 0-307-33660-3

Printed in China

A QUIRK PACKAGING BOOK

Edited by Sarah Scheffel
Technical editing by Mandy Moore
Design by Stephanie Stislow
Photographs by Bill Milne
Garments modeled by Meryl Finger (pages 36, 54, 59, 78, 80, 91, 96, 111, 128);
Laura Johnson (pages 32, 48, 59, 66, 69, 91, 100, 111, 120, 131, 142, 145);
Jackie Kristel (pages 44, 47, 59, 82, 84, 111, 112); Sandy May (pages 50, 59, 60,
63, 111, 116, 118, 131, 132, 136); and Natalie Venus Hull (pages 41, 59, 72, 74,
86, 89, 91, 92, 108, 111, 124, 131, 150, 153).
Illustrations by Erica Mulherin
Schematics and charts by Nancy Leonard

10 9 8 7 6 5 4 3

First Edition

Contents

Foreword

You may not believe this, but back in the day there was no Gap. There was no Lane Bryant, no Victoria's Secret. People actually made their own clothes and knit their own sweaters, so there was no such thing as a size 14 or a size 0 (one New York boutique will even sell you size 00 clothing if their size 0 is just too baggy for ya). Everything was fitted for and tailored to each specific body, however curvy or bony it was.

Cut to the modern day, when women are ready to throw themselves in front of trains (or under a plastic surgeon's knife), agonizing over the number on the label of their mass-produced pants. Some of us actually think this number has something to do with our personality! Ha!

Events conspired in the nineties and beyond to foster a wave of individuality and creativity, a longing for things unique and homemade. My friends dug out their Bedazzlers and started to craft and cook. And they began to knit. Everyone I knew started talking about skeins and row counts. Even Julia Roberts and Cameron Diaz picked up needles and began to knit. So did I. You know what happened?

Nothing.

I couldn't find attractive things to knit for ME. I'm a ripe, round size 18 to 20. The ponchos in most pattern books would come down to about . . . nipple height. Scarves looked like dishtowels thrown around my neck. And a buttoned cardigan looked more like a straight-jacket. Where were the patterns that not only fit big girls like me, but also flattered our shapes? Clearly, someone had dropped a stitch when it came to designing projects for women who wear a size 14 or larger.

That's when Jillian Moreno and Amy Singer stepped in. Frustrated with the knitting quo, they put their heads together to build body-flattering guidelines. Then they commissioned top designers to create this must-have collection of curve-friendly patterns. They chose fine yarns instead of the bulky, bumpy stuff. They accounted for pear shapes and apple shapes, big boobs and Buddha bellies. The results of their talent, experience, and creativity—and the brilliance of the designers they worked with—are right in these pages. Finally, we have beautiful, sexy, stylish patterns that fit and flatter women with real curves. Now Julia and Cameron's assistants, makeup artists, and friends—every girl with an itch to stitch—can join the A-listers' knitting circle.

So get to it, ladies! Make some sweaters! Let's show the world that women of all sizes can look fashionable, shapely, and innovative. While you knit and purl, I'm going to sit back and cackle at the wit of Jillian and Amy's words and admire the oh-so-pretty pictures in this book as all of your voluptuous friends will yearn to do, from the artistically impaired to the totally crafty.

Big Girl Knits is one small stitch for woman, and one big, beautiful sweater for womankind.

Stay stylish and strong,
Wendy Shanker
Author of *The Fat Girl's Guide to Life*
www.wendyshanker.com

chapter 1

The Secrets of Big Girl Knitting

Chances are if you're reading this book, you're fat. Join the club, and it's a big one. If the average American woman is a size 14, then a whole bunch of us are bigger. This includes knitters. Have you tried to find a flattering, funky, or even decent-fitting pattern lately? Ha!

If there's a butt load of us with a load of butt, why is it so hard to find good-looking patterns that fit us?

Here's a news flash about this book: nothing contained in these pages will make you look skinny. But we can make you look *good*.

See, most Big Girl knitters make stuff that doesn't fit them. Some of us knit fabric tents hoping to disguise anything that might poke out that we'd rather keep hidden. Some of us go the opposite direction, aiming for sexy by knitting skin tight sheaths that have no hope of being flattering. Heaven help those of us who've given up and only knit sweaters designed for men, just so we can get something big enough to go around us. We are not men! Even worse, overcompensating like this means we're using way more yarn than we have to. And yarn ain't cheap.

Most of us end up knitting sweater after sweater that clings in the wrong spot, sags, bags, and clearly doesn't make the most of our shapely shapes. Trying to hide your Big Girlness only makes you look fatter, because the garment you're wearing has no actual relation to your very personal body shape. So cut it out. The stuff in this book can be the first step in liberating your inner Big Girl; see how good you can look in your own handknits.

FIT AND YOUR BODY

Women's bodies go in and out. We've got curves and our knitting should wrap those curves lovingly—not hang like a sack or squeeze the stuffing out of us. Let your sweaters float and glide over your curves, not cling to them.

Oversized doesn't camouflage fat…it just swallows you up. People will point and say, "Look at the Big Girl being swallowed by her coat!" You look bigger in oversized garments because, for all anyone knows, you could be filling up the whole thing, even if you aren't.

Everything you knit to wear must have some shape. No dropped shoulders, no oversized anything, and no rectangles! While you're at it, throw away those leggings and big shirts left over from the eighties. They're over.

If you know your body and all its parts—how big they are, what you like, and what you don't—you can create shape by balancing between the good, the bad, and the wiggly. You are unique in all things, including your size and shape. If you knit sweaters that fit *you,* you are saying, "Hello, world! This is me. I look good, and check out this ass-kicking sweater I made."

So, what's the key to good fit? You need to have *and keep* a meticulous set of current measurements of your own body. If you haven't measured in a while, check out Chapter 3. It's nearly painless, especially if you make a party out of it.

USE COLORS THAT MAKE YOU GLOW

What color are you obsessed with? What color do people tell you looks great on you? What color makes you want to kick the world's ass? Screw black—knit with color!

If you're really not sure what colors rock your world or suit your skin tone, grab a couple of honest friends and have a little color party. Go to a yarn shop that has a big range of color in a smooth, non-variegated yarn—Cascade 220 is a great choice. Each of you grab skeins in five or six colors. Just fill a basket with what appeals to you without thinking too much. Include at least one set of colors you'd normally never go near, just to see. (It might be good to let the store staff know what you're doing—they'll be looking at you funny already.)

Find a patch of natural light and take turns holding colors up to your face—one skein on each side. Let your friends vote on the colors they like best on you, the ones that make your skin glow and your eyes sparkle. Rinse and repeat a couple of times. Take notes on the winners.

You don't need a mirror for this exercise, cause *you* don't get to vote. Why? **Ruts** and **relatives.**

We all get stuck in *color ruts.* Look at your wardrobe and your yarn stash…is it almost all one or two colors? They're the colors you feel safe with—your color rut. Sticking with the familiar may be easier, but being in any kind of rut is dull and depressing and does nothing to make you look the way you want to.

The main reason you don't get to judge your best colors are *those voices in your head: relatives.* The same voices that called you chunky, big boned, hefty, husky, plump, in *that* tone. You know that tone, especially if you've been a Big Girl your whole life. That "it's all about how you look, and you don't look right" tone. (We briefly pause this book to give all those people a one-fingered salute on behalf of Big Girls everywhere.)

The voices in your head that say things like "Fat girls shouldn't wear bright colors" and anything else narrow-minded or just plain wrong are what's steering you to the same colors again and again in the yarn shop. At worst they're the wrong colors for you, and at best they're BORING. That's why you don't get to pick this time. You are there to play with color with your yarn-loving friends, so let them steer you to hues and shades that make you look amazing.

Now buy a sweater's worth of the best color for you in a yarn you love and knit it. If you're like us, just a change of color will feel like a vacation.

OUR FAVORITE SPECIAL SOMEONE

At yarn stores, just like at clothing stores, there are people who are friends of Big Girls (FoBG). Worship them, memorize their work schedule, bring them coffee. These people get that the world does not come in just one size or shape. They will point out new patterns that come in your size; they will help you substitute yarn; if they are FoBG with math skills (the Holy Grail!), they can help resize a pattern you are in love with that calls a 40-inch bust XL.

FoBG are the ultimate yarn enablers, but you'll smile as you hand over your credit card because it means you've got extra ammunition to make sure your yarn dollars are well spent.

YARN

Speaking of yarn dollars, we think it's time for a few words on choosing yarn for Big Girls. Think about what kind of fibers you love working with. You're going to be touching and looking at them for a good stretch while you knit the thing, and it will be touching you for a long time while you wear it. Aside from the sensuality of the yarn you choose, there are some practical things to think about, too.

Bigger isn't better

If you learn only one thing from this book, this is it: **Big Girl Knits should use yarn four stitches to the inch or finer, period.** Do not put bulky, super-chunky-monkey garments on your Big Girl body. Thick yarn doesn't add inches to your silhouette, it

Hoist the Booby Flag!

Before you knit—before you even measure yourself—*buy a good bra.* Your sweaters will look better instantly. Look at the models in this book…no matter the size of their gazongas, they have one thing in common: each of them wears a really good bra. It makes a difference. Their girls sit up and bark!

Now it's your turn. Go get fitted at a specialty bra shop by a bossy lady who will feel you up. (Actually, she's just figuring out how you're built so she can get you the right size and style.) Or hit a major department store—their lingerie section will have fitting events throughout the year.

Spend as much money on a bra as you do on a sweater's worth of yarn, or more. Buy the cashmere equivalent of a bra. Your sweaters will fit better and you'll feel better. Your boobs aren't supposed to rest on your tum like they've had a hard day. Hoist the booby flag in a good bra and take a look! There's where your waist has been hiding!

adds *feet*—"Roll Out The Barrel" kind of width. Love chunky yarn? So make a blanket, make a scarf, make a hat, felt with it, or just knit something for someone else. Just don't *you* wear it.

Not so novel

Big expanses of shaggy, multi-strand, fluffy novelty yarns don't work on fluffy bods. Instead, use them as a detail or accent. Notice we did not say *scarf*? If you have boobs, streamlined scarves are great for creating a flattering vertical feeling, but fluffy scarves only make your chest look huge and hairy. "Me Tarzan, you Jane" huge and hairy.

If you want to wear a garment knit in novelty yarn, fall in love with ribbon. You'll get gorgeous color and interesting effects without turning into a puffball. Another secret—you can break the gauge rule and go a little thicker with ribbon yarn and still look good.

While we're touching on the fluffy side of yarn, fuzzy fibers like angora and mohair are best used:
a) sparingly
b) as one ingredient in a blend (so the yarn is less fuzzy)
c) as lace (to lighten the fabric *and* the look)
Yes. Any or all of the above.

Is it hot in here, or is it just me?

Not only do Big Girls look hot, we tend to run hot. Keep that in mind when choosing stuff to knit with. For indoor sweaters, look for blends. Adding a little silk, cotton, or microfiber to wool helps to cut down the *schvitz* factor. Or consider plant fiber yarns like cotton, flax, linen, and hemp—blended with microfiber or lycra to give them sproing. Plants are cool, man.

Girl, you've got to carry that weight (or wear it around your knees)

It takes a lot of yarn to make garments that fit us Big Girls. So when you're choosing yarn, you need to think about weight, as in "tote that barge" weight. Some fibers, like silk or fine wool, are inherently light. Others, like cotton, are just not. How many cotton sweaters do you own that have drooped to your knees over time? It's not your knitting or a mysterious gauge-morphing disease, it's the heft of pure cotton. So instead of using it straight up, look for a blend. Mixing cotton with microfiber not only lightens the load, it adds elasticity where we could sure use some.

Here's a reason to check yarn labels for more than the deal you're getting on yardage:

A long-sleeved, plain vanilla sweater with a finished chest measurement of 53 inches and a gauge of 5 stitches per inch uses about 1800 yards of yarn.

- Yarn A (100% cotton): 106 yards per 50 g
  17 skeins for our sweater.
  At 50 g per skein, that's **1.8 pounds of yarn.**
- Yarn B (cotton/microfiber blend): 160 yards per 50 g
  11 skeins for our sweater.
  At 50 g per skein, that's **1.1 pounds of yarn.**

At close to three quarters of a pound difference, which one will reach your knees first?

Microfiber Is Not Your Daddy's Leisure Suit

Microfiber is about how thin a fiber is, not the fiber it's made of. But all microfibers are man-made and most are made from polyester. Microfiber is the skinniest of all man-made fibers. Finer than the finest silk, some microfibers are thinner than hair. These tiny fibers, when blended with something like wool or cotton, lighten and strengthen the yarn and add elasticity. We like.

Color Hangover

Most store lighting sucks.

When you get seduced by a color in a yarn store, check it in natural light to see what it really looks like. Most stores have fluorescent lights that make everything look quite green, so go to the front of the shop where (hopefully) there's some daylight and double-check.

And always keep your receipts (or know the shop's return policy if you're buying online). If you're trying new colors, there's always a chance you may hate them in the morning and you don't want to be stuck with stuff you hate.

There's nothing worse than a color hangover.

Price and patience

Unless your yarn budget is bottomless (in which case we hate you), cost is always a factor when picking yarn. On average, we spend two to three times more than our skinny knitter sisters on yarn for each sweater. (So why don't more yarn store folk fall at our feet when we walk through the door? It baffles us.)

It can get ultra-expensive when you fall in love with cashmere/silk/angora/baby-animal-from-another-planet yarn. If you're really strapped for cash but still in love, try to find a way to use the super-expensive yarn as an accent—maybe for cuffs or a collar. That way you still get a treat and your wallet won't collapse from the strain.

We also have to ask ourselves how patient we are willing to be. Not many yarn shops carry two or three bags of a single yarn in the same color and dye lot, but that's often what we need. They'll probably have to special order it, which can take from a week to months, depending on the yarn company. So the flirty yarn that's making eyes at you from across the shop is not only asking "can you afford me?" but also "do you love me enough to wait for me?"

When it comes to yarn and money, we look at it this way: good yarn makes us happy. Wearing what we knit from the good yarn, especially if it makes us look amazing, makes us even more happy. Therefore, spending money on yarn contributes positively to our health. It's almost like a vitamin, really. Vitamin Y. Take 50 grams a day and repeat as needed.

We already said that Big Girls need to use yarn worsted weight or finer, but we'll say it again. It's that important.

Three Great Yarns for Big Girls

1. anything blended with lycra
2. microfiber on its own or as part of a blend
3. ribbon yarn, the Big Girl–friendly novelty

Three Not-So-Great Yarns for Big Girls

1. chunky
2. hairy
3. furry/fuzzy

chapter 2

My 20 ≠ Your 20

Every Big Girl is different. You and your best friend might both be a size 20, but if one of you has huge boobs and is relatively small elsewhere and the other one is all tummy and tush, it'd be pretty much a waste of time for you two to knit the same shape.

Let's say you both want to knit turtlenecks, which will look great on the belly/butt girl—the high neck will help balance her lower Bs. But on the boob girl, a high neck will magnify her rack, making it look like an immense loaf of home-baked bread stuck to her chest. There's no way a turtleneck will look good on both of you.

This is bound to cause resentment, and then you've killed a perfectly good friendship over knitwear.

Meet the B₃: Boobs, Belly, and Butt

There are three main areas that stick out, literally, when it comes to picking the right style to knit for you: they're your boobs, your belly, and your butt. We call them the B3.

To choose knitwear that will flatter your shape, it's all about balance, especially if one of your Bs is bigger, badder, and bouncier than the rest. You just have to know what you've got.

It's time. Stand in front of a mirror in your underwear and take a good look at you. **Which of your Bs stand out the most?** Be honest. If you need to, dig into Chapter 3, which talks more about measuring yourself. Once you've figured out which Bs you need to accommodate, you can use the tip sheets in this chapter to steer you to knitwear shapes that will suit *your* shape.

boobs   belly   butt

THE B3 SYSTEM

Here's how it works: If you've got big boobs, but nothing else stands out, you want to choose design details from the boob section. If you have big boobs and a big butt, but your belly is understated, then focus on those two sections of the book.

Every pattern in this book comes with B3 icons. For example, if the boob icon appears at the top of a pattern, it means that the pattern will look great on a boob girl. So once you know your Bs, browse the patterns by icon for the styles that will suit your personal body best. Some patterns work for more than one B.

Our goal is to make the most of your overall shape and each of your Bs without making any individual B look bigger than it needs to. No system is perfect…and no shape suits every *body*. But following the principles we talk about for each of the Bs are the keys to finally choosing styles to knit that will make you feel *and* look good.

Boobs, breasts,
or rack?
Cut it low and
close to showcase
your stack.

GOT RACK?

Boob girls are lucky. Your rack gives you an element of balance on top for whatever may follow down below. So you can handle some body groping–knits that follow your body contours closely.

The key to beautifying your boobage is to **show some chest skin.** There is no point in trying to hide it. If you wear a high neck (crew or turtle), it creates the image of one huge boob instead of two shapely boobies. So **don't knit turtlenecks.** Go for deep Vs and Us, scoops, and sweetheart necklines, and show the girls off! For coats and jackets, a deep V that ends below your boobs is most flattering, otherwise your girls look trapped and flat. Long shawl collars frame your face *and* boobs—yum. Just don't get into fussy detail in the boob region; they're quite enough on their own.

Showing off your waist, even by an inch, makes a huge difference to your overall silhouette. It also helps to eliminate all of the extra bunched-up fabric on the back part of your waist. Don't forget about that spot right under your boobs, which is now visible because you're wearing a kick-ass bra. It's usually the smallest part of your torso and it's a nice spot to accentuate, either through fit or color.

A coat or jacket that's **fitted at the waist and flared at the hem** is the most flattering look for boob girls, and gives you a little Marilyn thing to boot. Empire waists are great as long as the fabric flows from the slimmer spot below your boobs, not from the top of them…otherwise you look pregnant!

Where does it all end when it comes to hemlines? Anywhere that suits the rest of you, as long as you **don't show tummy skin.** That just adds to the visual impression your already impressive boobs give, making them look even bigger.

NECKLINES
- U, V, scoop, or sweetheart necklines
- go deep…right to your cleavage
- wide and open
- off-shoulder or strapless
- deep V-necked coats and jackets
- long, slim shawl collars

WAISTLINES
- fitted styles including corsets, prop-erly placed empire waists, wraps
- even an inch indent looks good

BOTTOMLINES
- pick a length that suits your bottom half
- flared hems and fitted waists give you bonus curves

OVERALL
- follow your curves more closely
- think fit and flare
- wear cardigans and jackets open for a vertical line

DON'T YOU DARE
- turtle your neck
- crop and show tummy
- go boxy
- do A-line or tunic tops

All Hail the Wrap!

The wrap sweater is the friend of all Big Girls. It creates the look of a waist where one may not be; it's got an attractive diagonal line thing going on in the boob area that creates interest if you have no boobs to speak of or is hellishly flattering if you do have serious boobage; and it fits you right every time, since you can adjust it to suit you. Knit a wrap.

Belly, pooch, or tummy? Work it up high and down low to look yummy.

DO THE BUDDHA

Belly girls and their butt sisters get something that boob girls long for: all the interesting, **funky necklines and wild collars** you can knit. To balance your belly, you get to knit high necks, low necks, two-foot lapels, chest pockets. Anything interesting. Or go long. Details at the neckline, lapels, button bands, or the bottom of a longer hemline draw the eye up or down, balancing la belly.

You don't have a waistline? Yes, you do. It just may not go in the direction you want. You want to create the impression of a waist, but lightly, with a feather touch...certainly nothing as crude as a grope.

You could also go **straight and longish** (past the biggest part of your tum) with a tunic. Remember that balance is everything: *short and straight* is a box ☹, *longish and straight* is a tunic ☺.

An **A-line sweater** is a gorgeous way to show off a yarn you really love, since it gives you bonus yardage to play with. Most importantly, the inverted-V shape mimics your shape without clinging where it shouldn't. But A-lines must stop at the right place, so don't keep A-lining all the way to the bottom of your hip. Then you're back into the tent thing, and we're not going there.

If you stop a sweater in the wrong place, it can be a big deal. Instead, you want your sweaters to slip out of notice, not act as a flashing arrow that says, "Hey! Look at the biggest part of my body!" So make sure you **stop below your biggest bump,** not in the middle of it. That streamlines your silhouette all the way down. And trust us, you don't want ribbing at the hem that pulls the whole garment in. That's another flashing arrow that calls attention to your tum. Think straight down, except for gentle waist shaping.

NECKLINES
- anything, especially if it's interesting

WAISTLINES
- think waist-creating shapes like corsets, wraps, and properly placed empire waists
- straight tunics
- A-line flyaways—shirts or jackets—that end just past your biggest bump

BOTTOMLINES
- high hip or hipbone
- knee-length fitted coats
- shirt tails
- tunic length

OVERALL
- end after biggest bump
- cover, don't cling
- think semi-fitted A-line or rectangular, not square

NO, NO, NO
- cropped
- boxy
- tight through the middle

Butt, back, or booty? Fit and flare will make the most of your patooty.

1 CUSHY TUSHY?

Big butts come in a few flavors: the ones you can set a tray on (they jut out straight at the back) or the others that knock stuff over as they go past (they're wide and hang low). They often have a couple of friends along for company—big thighs, saddlebags. The idea with a butt—high or low variety—is to gently **smooth the line of the tush and draw the eye upward for balance.**

Following the same principles of redirection as our belly sisters, butt girls get to play with fun stuff everywhere *but* their butts. So think about really interesting necklines, and **put detail and embellishment up high** (to even out your down low). And from our boob sisters, borrow the idea of fit and flare. Work your waist and boobs, then flare out smoothly past your butt. Show off what you've got upstairs; even if it's not your dream chest, it will be dreamy.

Now we get to the bottom line: your bottom. Where you stop a garment is more important than for any other Big Girl. You've gotta stop either before you get to it or totally cover it with a sexy, sleek line. If you stick a hem in the middle of your generous tush, you double its size. It's like a flashing sign that says "Look at both of my butts!" So **look for jackets that end past your end,** or go way long. And please, think ease, not E-A-S-E. Just enough to skim, not enough to hide a fleet of battleships. *Too much* is *not* a good thing for Big Girls.

NECKLINES
- big lapels
- square necks
- mandarin collars
- anything interesting!

WAISTLINES
- wraps
- define your waist, even if just a hint

BOTTOMLINES
- either stop before you get to it or totally cover it
- if you want long, fit your waist, skim your tush, and go way long

OVERALL
- semi-fitted or fit and flare
- no booty groping—skim and smooth

NO WAY
- bottom ribbing
- butt-bisecting hemlines
- straight tunics

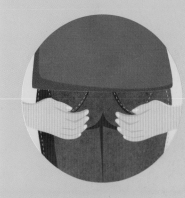

Stamp Out Knitwear Butt Cuppage!

Join our crusade! There should be no ribbing at the bottom of your knitted things. Nothing that pulls the sweater *in.* The only thing cupping your butt should be your honey's hands.

WHAT IF ALL YOUR Bs ARE BODACIOUS?

If two or all three of your Bs are remarkable, how do you choose what to knit? It's all up to you and how you feel about your body.

Let's say you've got big boobs and a big belly. You love your boobs, but your belly…not so much. Go for a deep scoop-necked empire-waisted sweater. The scoop flatters the boobage and the empire waist directs attention away from the belly.

If you're all Bs from the waist down, focus on the belly rules…but make sure to pick your hemline detailing from the butt department. Love your butt? Stop above it. Don't want to show it off? Skim past it.

Maybe you've got all three Bs at full volume. You don't care much for the top two, but love showing off your booty? Try a modest V or scoop neck (showing enough skin to visually separate the girls), add a whisper of waist shaping, and end your sweater right above your butt. Want more butt? Add detail at the bottom of the sweater—maybe some lace or an interesting hem treatment. If you'd rather direct attention up, go with the boob rules instead.

BOTTOMS FOR YOUR BOOTY: THE BONUS B

Knitted pants and skirts are popping up everywhere. Why should Big Girls get left out?

Pants

Balance is the key with pants. Whatever you put on your bottom, you're trying to balance what's above. And what's above is likely quite big.

The two **best pant shapes for Big Girls are wide-ish and straight or boot cut/flared. No tapering,** unless you want to look like an ice cream cone. And NO leggings, none, ever. No.

Skirts

The **best shape for most Big Girls is the A-line skirt**—anything from barely flared A to capital A. If you're a hippy hipster, you need the balance of a wider line at the bottom of your bottom. Your A-line doesn't need to be crisp and stiff. Just look at the skirt—the hem should be noticeably wider than the waist. The outward flare of an A-line from your waist to your knees (or whatever length you like and looks good with your legs) is flowy and flattering and kinda disguises what's going on underneath.

If you have a straight-back butt with no sidesaddle friends, you can wear straight and bias skirts, too.

Thigh friction can be managed with your choice of shaper garment—check the lingerie department. Even with the lightest lycra (minimal holding power), they'll smooth-coat your thighs so you don't start fires from the rubbing. Hate compression? Try cotton boxer shorts. Who'll know?

A big belly or butt can pull your skirt up so your hem sits too short in the front or back. So compensate by adding vertical inches only where you need them. Yes, one side of your skirt CAN be longer than the other because that way it will look perfectly even on your non-symmetrical bod.

OTHER BODY BITS
Chins

Does your chin have friends? (It would be lonely to be a chin.) Elongate! **Show lots of skin between your neck and chin** with deep Us, Vs, scoops, and square necks. Unless, of course, you *want* that neckless-linebacker look.

Arms

We are yelling now: **Don't do dropped.** Dropped and modified-dropped shoulder designs add inches to your upper half. Why add visual width that's not actually there? Worse, the sloppy dropped shoulder line creates a horizontal arrow pointing right at your boobs. Who needs that?

dropped   set-in   raglan

So what do you knit? **Set-in sleeves look best on Big Girls** cause they give stable structure to a garment and create a vertical line that is closer to your real body shape. Raglans can work if you don't have huge shoulders. (Raglans make your shoulders look bigger.) Otherwise, they're worth considering cause they give good diagonal and that draws the eye back to your face, where it belongs.

Will you go sleeveless? Well, how do you feel about your arms? If you hate your arms, no number of gorgeous knitted tanks are going to change your mind. On the fence about your arms? Make a tank and wear a jacket or cardigan over it; then another day, wear a shawl over a tank for a while, gradually easing your arms out into the world. You may find you're happy with peek-a-boo arms. Cultivate a collection of modern twin sets...tanks plus wraps.

A WORD ON ACCESSORIES

Shawls and wraps

Think big shawls for big girls. Rectangular wraps for the skinny masses are usually in the neighborhood of 24 x 72 inches, including fringe. But fringe doesn't cover flesh, unless you pin the edges of the fringe to your boobs. (Ow.) **Try 30 x 90 inches.** If you're a super-queen, go bigger. You deserve to be generously wrapped in merino or silk or cashmere. (Hey, no one said it was cheap being a Big Girl.)

For circular or triangular shawls, follow the same rules you'd use when picking sweater or jacket length. The back of the shawl has to hit the right spot on you, and it shouldn't be your biggest spot.

Scarves

Scarves rock. They're quick and easy, they don't use much yarn, they can be immensely satisfying to make, and everyone, even non-knitters, notices them.

Scarves rock Big Girls because they are great for balancing all of the Bs. They're like a big vertical lasso tying all your Bs together. Keep in mind for wear-all-day scarves versus keep-me-toasty scarves, you want fine, light yarn, nothing that adds bulk (no fluffy, fuzzy, or chunky). And boob girls will have to make theirs a little longer to ride over the curves.

Bags

You're a Big Girl, so **don't carry a teeny bag**—the contrast makes you look bigger. Plus, you can't fit anything in it. Try 12 or 16 inches wide. Go to the purse section of your favorite store and try out different bag sizes against your bod in the mirror. See what we mean?

Why Do You Want to Knit This Sweater?

Is it the color, the yarn, the model wearing it, or maybe just the collar?

Catalog the sweater: What will look good with your parts, what won't? What do you need to alter to make it better for you? Still love it? Do the math (okay, just *look* at the math). Are you willing and able to make the necessary adjustments?

If you can't find the exact pattern you have pictured in your head, design it yourself. There are people you know who will help you (knitting friends, yarn shop FoBG). There are books and classes to learn from. You can do it.

Once you find a pattern that works for you, knit it again and again. The pattern is your base recipe. Pick different colors, use the basic shape and add a stitch pattern, or change the collar and cuffs. Split a pullover into a cardigan, lengthen or shorten the hem. Each variation will be totally new, but you can relax and enjoy the knitting cause you know your sweater will fit when you're done.

OTHER STUFF TO OBSESS ABOUT BEFORE YOU START KNITTING

Which way does it feel?

Try for a vertical feeling in your knitting. Your knitting creates all kinds of lines on your body: Garments don't necessarily need stripes to have verticalness. Color patterns, texture stitches, details like collars and button bands, diagonals, variegated yarns, overall shape…all of these create lines. If you're a Big Girl, you want vertical ones.

It's usually easy to spot hidden horizontals. You look at pattern and say "I wouldn't want that row of pockets (or other offensive horizontal element) stretched across my (insert appropriate B here)."

If you can't tell if a particular element is more vertical than horizontal, squint and look again. A blurry view will help you spot the vertical versus horizontal feeling in the pattern. Don't study every detail—it will make you crazy.

Beware the lifestyle trap!

Take a good look at a sweater you want to knit. Do you love the sweater or the life the model is living in the photo? Think about it before you cast on, cause nothing you knit will get you a Vespa or a villa.

You know those rules we gave you?

Find a rule to break. There are so many rules in life and when you're a Big Girl it's worse because you get extra life rules handed to you by other people. So pick a rule from our list or anyone else's and don't do it, or do the opposite. Then dance around with your iPod cranked. We love this.

Big Girls' Top Ten Things to Knit

1. **Sweaters* that skim the shape of your body. You want tents? Join a circus.**

2. **Wrap-style sweaters.** The Holiest Grail in Big Girl knitting. Wraps can define a waist, create the illusion of waist where none exists, and cover a belly. What's not to love?

3. **Finer-gauge yarn** (we're talking worsted weight or finer). Bulky yarn makes bodies bulkier.

4. **V-necks.** Show off those luscious boobies if you've got 'em. Create a flattering vertical if you don't.

5. **Shaped sweaters.** Same riff as the wrap. Defines your shape. Saves on yarn, too.

6. **Sweaters that end before or after your widest part.** If a sweater ends in the middle of your big belly, it will look like you have two bellies. Nice.

7. **Vertical elements.** Look to see if any patterning is sneakily creating horizontals —Fair Isle bands over big butts, patterned yokes over big boobs.

8. **Detail that accentuates the parts of your body you love.** Love your boobies? Nestle them in lace and ruffles. Skinny waist? Shape all of your sweaters to death, add color, buttons, anything that screams "Look at me and my skinny waist." Do you have beautiful, graceful hands and wrists? Knit your sleeves to three-quarters or bracelet length; add cuffs, beads, ruffles.

9. **Any damn color that makes you happy.** Black is not magic. Black does not make you look thin; black does not give you a shape. Black makes you look like a fat girl wearing black.

10. **Knit what you love.** Wear what you knit—you'll be fabulous.

* We say sweaters, but we mean anything you knit to wear.

chapter 3

This Is the Part Where You Get Measured

Two things above all others will ensure that your sweater really fits you:
- accurate gauge (in the calculating AND the knitting)
- knitting to your *current* measurements

What's current? No, not the measurements you remember from college, from before you had kids, from fourth grade, or from some time in the future when you lose 10 pounds from who-knows-where on your body. You need measurements that come directly from your body *now* to have a sweater that fits you *now*.

GAUGE

Just a couple words about doing a gauge swatch: you must. It makes everything turn out like you meant it to. I know you just want to start the freaking sweater already so you can wear it on the weekend. But chances are you won't be wearing it—you'll be hanging out by the frog pond ripping it and starting over again, or stuffing it into the bad project black hole in the back of your closet. Because it'll end up being totally the wrong size for you.

Again with the lectures, but it's important: four measly rows do not constitute a gauge swatch. **Aim for a 4 x 4–inch swatch, bind off (yes, bind off! It makes your gauge reading more accurate), and measure it on a hard surface like a table,** not draped over your thigh or the arm of your couch. (Ha! Caught you!) Check the gauge in several different parts of the swatch to get a consensus. You've gone to the rather minimal trouble of knitting the swatch, so you might as well aim for reasonable accuracy in your numbers.

Periodically check your gauge as you knit the project. There's a not-so-rare yet little-mentioned knitting disease called Incredible Changing Gauge Syndrome (ICGS). It happens when you get into the knitting swing of things. You start to relax and so can your gauge. Or you're knitting against time and the deadline approacheth; you're tense and tight and so is your gauge. Just recheck your gauge from time to time. Look, you're already obsessively measuring the length to know when to stop, so taking a sec to recheck your gauge isn't going to kill you.

EASE

You may be as easy as a Sunday morning, but you don't want all of your sweaters to be.

Ease is the wiggle room between you and your sweater; it can range from skin tight to sack attack. It's up to you (and maybe a few of your close personal friends) to figure out what you like and what looks good on you.

A quick way to start is to measure you and then measure a finished sweater that fits like you want a sweater to fit. Compare the measurements. If the chest of the sweater is 4 inches larger than your chest measurement, that's the ease you like—4 inches.

Here's a secret: your ease doesn't have to be the same all over. Love your boobies, hate your tum? So have 1 inch of ease over your boobs, 3 inches over your belly. Remember, you're making this for you, so make it exactly how *you* want it to fit.

How Easy Are You?

According to the Craft Yarn Council, there's a way to categorize the amount of ease you like.

VERY CLOSE FITTING: Actual measurement or smaller
CLOSE FITTING: add 1 to 2 inches (2.5 to 5 cm)
STANDARD FITTING: add 2 to 4 inches (5 to 10 cm)
LOOSE FITTING: add 4 to 6 inches (10 to 15 cm)

6 inches
4 inches
2 inches

CHOOSING A SIZE TO KNIT

When you're choosing which size to knit in a pattern, remember that sizes mean nothing. They're only labels so you know which bit of the pattern to follow. The pattern may say L[1X, 2X, 3X], but it might as well be Blue[Red, Pink, Purple]. Actually, that would be quite festive. No, you've got to look at the finished measurements to choose your size. And you get to do this every time you choose a new pattern to knit. This is why schematics (the little drawings of the thing you're knitting with numbers all over them) are so important.

But not all patterns provide schematics (bad, bad, patterns). So choose a size based on the finished bust measurement and customize the rest to suit your shape. How? Check out Chapter 4 for some methods and math to make a straight sweater fit you better. (If you're knitting bottoms, use the finished hip measurement to pick a size instead.)

And one last note: the finer the yarn you use, the more built-in ease you get. Finer = flowier! So 4 inches of ease in a fingering-weight cardigan might be too much, but 4 inches of ease in a worsted-weight cardigan may be just right.

HOW TO GET YOUR MEASUREMENTS

You need a friend to help you measure. There are several reasons why you can't measure yourself:

1. **Accuracy.** These numbers need to be accurate, or why are you even bothering to take them? The measuring tape needs to be placed in the right spot. The tape has to be held at a correct and consistent tension. *All* the measurements need to be taken, not just the ones you feel like doing.
2. **Physical limitations.** Unless you have 12-foot-long detachable arms, you can't tell us that you can properly measure your own back. You're attached to your limbs and eyes, so use someone else's to measure you.
3. **Fire factor** as in "liar, liar, pants on fire." You will lie. We all do. Your measurements need to be accurate to get a great fit, not viewed through self-soothing rose-colored glasses. Your friend will be honest for you.

Also, try to measure yourself every year, not just once in a blue moon. Why? We expand and contract in all kinds of ways all the time. (And because gravity is a bitch.) Your sense of style may change; you may want your sleeves longer and your skirts shorter. Fresh measurements help you get what you want every time.

The measuring process

1. Wear your best sweater bra, a tight tank or T-shirt, and leggings or yoga pants.
2. Tie a piece of waste yarn snug (but not tight) in two places: one around your waist and one under your arms where you want your armhole to end, between your armpit crease and the top of your bra.
3. Mark your nipples and the end of your shoulder bones with sticky dots.
4. Start at the top of your body and work down, following the measurement chart on page 21.
5. Don't hold your breath while being measured.
6. Measure your favorite sweater when you're done and add its numbers to the chart at the end of this chapter.

Throw a Measuring Party!

Why not play while you measure? Invite enough girls for it to be fun, but not so many that you run out of time to measure everyone. And you must invite only people who feel comfortable enough with each other to run around nearly naked. This is no time to make new friends.

Everyone should bring:
- Measuring gear (see page 19)
- Favorite-fitting sweater to measure
- Sense of humor…you'll all be wearing nipple dots!
- Favorite beverage
- Snacks to share
- Knitting to work on/show off
- New yarny purchases to show off

Hostess with the mostess can provide:
- Music
- Appropriate beverages or mixers for your crowd
- Stuff to eat off and drink from
- Extra measuring kits for the goofballs who forget theirs

The quickest way to get all the measuring done is to work in pairs, each measuring the other. If there is a particularly detail-oriented (completely anal) knitter or two among your group, you could try and persuade them to measure everyone. There's more time to socialize this way. You may want to give your measurers a little giftie when it's all done, because they don't get to play as much. (How about a gift certificate to the best yarn shop in town?)

If you are a designated measurer, no adult beverages until you're finished!

What else is fun at a measuring party?
- Knitting door prizes
- Yarn swap
- Ugliest knitted thang contest

Some ground rules:
- No cameras unless everyone agrees—no one wants to be surprised with a photo of herself sporting nipple dots on your blog.
- If you are a designated measurer, ask your measuree if she wants her numbers called out as you go—some do, some don't.

My Measurements

NAME: **DATE:**

Chest/Waist:

Chest circumference **[B]:**

Front Chest (horizontally over boobs to where side seam would be):

Back (horizontally across back to where side seams would be):

Nipple distance (nipple dot to nipple dot) **[ND]:**

Armpit depth (top of shoulder to armpit crease):

Preferred armhole depth (from top of your shoulder to just above your bra strap) :

Waist (waist string) **[W]:**

Shoulder to front waist
(shoulder to waist string *over* boobs):

Shoulder to back waist:

Waist to armhole:

Upper length (waist string to bottom of bra band) **[UL]**

Side length (favorite sweater length, hem to bottom of bra band) **[SL]:**

Preferred sweater length, from shoulder to hem:

Lower Length (favorite sweater length hem to waist string) **[LL]:**

Front Length (favorite sweater length hem to shoulder over boobs) **[FL]:**

Back Length (favorite sweater length hem to shoulder over back) **[BL]:**

Shoulder dot to shoulder dot [cross back]:

Hips:

High hip **[H]:**

Low hip (saddlebaggage):

Arms:

Upperarm:

Wrist:

Forearm:

Sleeve lengths (measured from shoulder dot):
ss: ¾: ls:

Tank strap width:

Accessories

Foot

Foot length:

Foot circumference:

Above ankle circumference:

Calf circumference at favorite top of sock length:

Favorite sock height:

Hand

Hand circumference:

Wrist circumference:

Middle finger length:

Middle finger circumference:

Wrist to fingertip:

Other

Head circumference:

Preferred scarf length:

Preferred shawl width and length:
W: L:

Favorite sweater measurements

TYPE: ☐ pullover   ☐ cardigan   ☐ jacket   ☐ coat   ☐ vest   ☐ other:

Length (shoulder to hem):

Bust:

Waist:

Hip:

Sleeve length:

Sleeve width at widest point:

Neckline type:

Neckline depth:

Neckline width:

Amount of ease:
at Bust:

at Waist:

at Hips:

chapter 4

The Two Indispensable Adaptations for Big Girls

What follows are our favorite tools for customizing the stuff we knit, and we don't mind sharing.

We'd love to give you a no-math way to add shape to your knitting, but it doesn't exist. However, we have done our best to simplify and streamline the concepts so you'll be able to understand what you're doing and why.

So grab your measurement chart, a calculator, and a little caffeine and let's rock some adaptations!

ADAPTATION 1: WAIST SHAPING
What is it?
Reducing the measurement at the waist of a sweater to create a curvier silhouette.

What can it do for you?
Create or define a waist; create curves from a cube.

How it works
Waist shaping has 4 parts:
1. Calculate number of stitches to indent at the waist
2. Decrease that number of stitches ending 1 inch below waist
3. Knit straight (no shaping) for 2 inches to define the waist
4. Increase the same number of stitches to just below armhole

Special skills needed
None. It's just decreasing and increasing!

Our girlfriend wants some shape.
Our Big Girl girlfriend has found a pattern that she loves. It's got great design details, but it's a nasty box shape that won't suit her.

The sweater is sized 50 inches all the way up and down. Like a tube sock with sleeves.

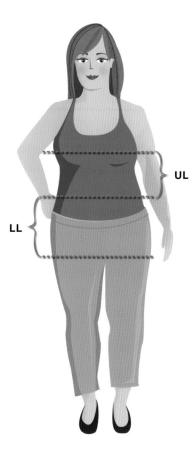

She has a set of her recent measurements, she knows her favorite amount of ease, and since she's swatched already, she has all the information she needs for the yarn she's using. She plugs it into her chart.

What is it?	Secret code	Our girlfriend's numbers
Body Stuff		
Waist (yours)	W	43"
Ease (your favorite ease)	E	3"
Ideal Sweater Waist: **W+ E**	ISW	46"
Sweater Stuff		
Stitch gauge per inch	S	4
Row gauge per inch	R	6
Lower Length (hem to waist)	LL	7"
Upper Length (waist to armhole)	UL	9"
Lower length −1" (for half of the 2" straight at the waist: decreases worked over this measurement)	LL-1	6"
Upper length −1" (for the other half: increases worked over this measurement)	UL-1	8"
Sweater Waist (from the pattern, it's probably the same as the finished Bust measurement)	SW	50"
Difference at Waist: **SW–ISW**	DW	4"

Remember, the 4 parts of waist shaping are:

1. Calculate number of stitches to indent at the waist
2. Decrease those stitches from sweater hem to 1 inch below waist
3. Knit straight (no shaping) for 2 inches to define the waist
4. Increase the same number of stitches to just below armhole

Step 1: First let's figure out how many stitches she needs to decrease.

$$DW \times S = TDS \text{ (total decrease stitches)}$$

4 inches x 4 stitches per inch = 16 stitches

Where do those decreases happen? In a sweater, you usually decrease at the side edges of the front and back pieces – so that's 4 edges.

$$TDS \div 4 = TDSe \text{ (total decrease stitches per edge)}$$

16 ÷ 4 = 4 decreases per edge

Step 2: How many rows does she decrease over?

$$LL\text{-}1 \times R = \text{number of rows to decrease over}$$

6 inches x 6 rows per inch = 36 rows

How often does she do the actual decreasing?

$$R \div TDSe = \text{decrease interval}$$

36 rows ÷ 4 = 9 rows

So she'll decrease **1 stitch at each edge every 9 rows 4 times.**

When working a decrease row every 9 rows, work 8 rows, then a decrease row. The decrease row will be the <u>last</u> row of the 9 rows.

Step 3 is easy! She'll knit 2 inches straight (no shaping) to define the waist. So will you when it's your turn.

On to **Step 4:** Increase stitches from waist to just below armhole. She'll increase the same number of stitches as she's just decreased: 16, or 4 stitches per edge.

To figure how many rows she has to increase over, it's just like Step 2:

$$UL\text{-}1 \times R = \textit{number of rows to increase over}$$
8 inches x 6 rows per inch = 48 rows

$$\textit{Number of rows to increase over} \div TDSe = \textit{increase interval}$$
48 rows ÷ 4 increases = 12 rows

So she increases **1 stitch each side every 12 rows 4 times.**

When working a increase row every 12 rows, work an increase row, then 11 rows. The increase row will be the <u>first</u> row of the 12 rows.

Here's how this part looks in the chart:

Convert inches to stitches	**DW x S = TDS**	4 × 4 = 16
Total Decrease Stitches per edge	**TDS ÷ 4 = TDSe**	16 ÷ 4 = 4
Decrease at each edge every __th row	**(LL-1 x R) ÷ TDSe**	(6 × 6) ÷ 4 = 9
Knit straight for 2"		2"
Increase at each edge every __th row	**(UL-1 x R) ÷ TDSe**	(8 × 6) ÷ 4 = 12

Even Amy gets this, and she's totally numbers impaired. So you can do it too!

Now here's a complete chart for you to use! Photocopy it and fill it in for any sweater you want to modify.

What is it?	Secret code	My numbers
Body Stuff		
Waist (yours)	W	
Ease (your favorite ease)	E	
Ideal Sweater Waist: **W+ E**	ISW	
Sweater Stuff		
Stitch gauge per inch	S	
Row gauge per inch	R	
Lower Length (hem to waist)	LL	
Upper Length (waist to armhole)	UL	
Lower length –1 (for half of the 2" straight at the waist – decreases worked over this measurement)	LL-1	
Upper length –1 (for the other half – increases worked over this measurement)	UL-1	
Sweater Waist (from the pattern, it's probably the same as the finished Bust measurement)	SW	
Difference at Waist: **SW–ISW**	DW	
Convert inches to stitches	DW x S = TDS	
Total Decrease Stitches per edge	TDS ÷ 4 = TDSe	
Decrease at each edge every __th row	(LL-1 x R) ÷ TDSe	
Knit straight for 2"	2"	2"
Increase at each edge every __th row	(UL-1 x R) ÷ TDSe	

ADAPTATION 2: SHORT ROWS

What are they?

Short rows are knitted rows that are narrower than the piece you're knitting. How the heck do you do that? You start working a row, but don't go all the way to the end. You turn your work, knit back almost to the end, turn, etc. It might sound nuts, but it's really quite clever. You're building little wedges of extra knitting.

These wedges create extra fabric in a specific spot without lengthening the whole sweater. Short rows can be used to make space for any bumps or curves you've got, like your hips, tum, shoulders, heels…but in this particular learning experience, we're talking boobs only—short-row bust darts.

What can they do for you?

Short rows make room for your boobs without changing any other part of the sweater. Imagine you're wearing an otherwise well-fitting sweater that has no shaping at the chest. If you've got a C cup or bigger, the front of that sweater is riding up higher than the back and you're constantly yanking at it, aren't you?

What if you could magically cut open a slit in the sweater from the far side of one boob across the front to the far side of the other boob – but not as far as the side seam. Your boobs could escape for a breath of fresh air, and the sweater hem would drop down to where it's supposed to be. Now mentally fill that boob-space slit with more knitting – just in the front, like a superhero booby mask. That's what short rows do. They're the superhero of all boob girls.

How they work

Short rows have 7 parts:

1. Figuring where on the sweater to begin working the dart (somewhere between the hem and armhole)
2. Calculating bust-dart depth
3. Calculating bust-dart width
4. Calculating the number of turning points
5. Calculating when to make those turns
6. Knitting the little suckers so gaps don't show where you turned your work
7. Making the gap-hiding bumps disappear

Short rows work magic for you.

Special skills needed

A method to knit short rows.
There are many; we're using the Wrap & Turn method (W&T).

How to Wrap & Turn:

Work up to the spot where you need to begin your short rows.

1. With the yarn in front, slip the next stitch to your R needle. [A]
2. Bring the yarn to the back, passing it in front of the slipped stitch. [B]
3. Slip the stitch from the R needle back to the L needle. [C]
4. Turn your piece and prepare to work back in the direction you just came from.

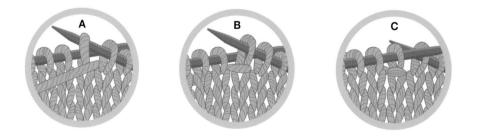

That little wrappy bit keeps a hole from forming when you turn your piece and work your way back, but it leaves a little bump on the bottom of the wrapped stitch so we need…

…A method to make the little bumps from wrapping disappear

After you finish creating the wedge of extra fabric with your short rows, you go back to knitting normally, across full rows. But before you can do that, you're going to have to deal with each wrapped stitch you've made to keep the transition invisible. When you encounter a stitch that has been wrapped, here's what you do: pick up the wrap [it's the horizontal bar snugged around the base of the vertical stitch], place it on the left needle, and knit [or purl] it together with the stitch it had previously wrapped. Ta-da!

OUR GIRLFRIEND IS A BOOB GIRL

We've got another girlfriend who wants to make a sweater that fits over her bountiful boob area. She is terrified of the words 'short rows' but is willing to try if we hold her hand. We'll hold yours too.

She has all of her pertinent numbers, so she slides them into the chart like so:

What is it?	Secret code	Our girlfriend's numbers
Body Stuff		
Front Length (shoulder to front waist over your boobs)	**FL**	26"
Back Length (shoulder to back waist)	**BL**	22"
Front/Back Difference: **FL–BL**	**FBD**	4"
Side length (hem to bottom of your bra band (1 or 2" below armhole)	**SL**	12"
Nipple Distance (horizontal distance between nipples)	**ND**	10"
Tasteful Nipple Distance (so short rows don't peak on your nipples – trust us!): **ND** + 2"	**TND**	12"
Sweater Stuff		
Stitch gauge per inch	**S**	4
Row gauge per inch	**R**	6
Sweater Bust circumference	**SB**	48"

Now we follow the steps:

Step 1: Figuring where on the sweater to begin working the short rows (they go between the hem and armhole)
This one is easy. Knit your sweater front until you reach **SL.** This is usually between 1 and 2 inches below the armhole shaping. This is where your short rows go. On our Big Girl, **SL** is 12 inches.

Step 2: Calculating bust-dart depth (BDD)
How tall (how many rows) will our Big Girl's short row section be?
It needs to fill the difference between **FL** and **BL** so her sweater hangs evenly on all sides.

$$FL - BL = BDD$$
26 inches – 22 inches = 4 inches
Her short row section needs to fill 4 inches of height.

Convert that distance to rows:
$$BDD \times R = BDR \text{ (Bust Dart Rows)}$$
4 inches x 6 rows per inch = 24 rows
That means she'll do 24 short rows to fill in that 4 inches.

Step 3: Calculating bust-dart width (BDW)
$$SB \div 2 = FSW \text{ (Front Sweater Width)}$$
48 inches ÷ 2 = 24 inches

The front of her sweater will be 24 inches wide. She doesn't care about the back, since she doesn't need boob room there!

The **TND** (Tasteful Nipple Distance) is the area at the center front of the sweater, from nipple to nipple and a little beyond. All the short rows cover this area, and all turning points happen outside this area, in the bust darts at the side edges of the sweater. To figure out how much width she has for each bust dart, she subtracts the **TND** from the **FSW:**
$$FSW - TND \div 2 = BDW \text{ (Bust Dart Width)}$$
(24 inches – 12 inches) ÷ 2 = 6 inches

And then she converts that measurement to stitches:
$$BDW \times S = BDS \text{ (Bust Dart Stitches)}$$
6 inches x 4 stitches per inch = 24 stitches

Each bust dart will be 6 inches or 24 stitches wide at the widest point.

Step 4: Calculating the number of Turning Points (TP)
Another easy one. Short rows are always worked in pairs (one on the RS for the right boob and one on the WS for the left boob), so she divides her number of short rows by 2 to get the number of turning points she needs.
$$BDR \div 2 = TP$$
24 rows ÷ 2 = 12 turning points on each side

Step 5: Calculating when to make your turns
Each pair of short rows has to be a little shorter than the pair before it. How many stitches shorter will each row be?

$$BDS \div TP = SRI \; \textit{(Short Row Increments)}$$
24 stitches ÷ 12 turns = 2 stitches

The short rows will be worked in 2-stitch increments. This means that each short row will end 2 stitches before the end of the previous short row, on each side. In other words, each short row will be 2 stitches shorter than the last.

Step 6: Knitting the little suckers so gaps don't show where you turned your work.
Our girlfriend had worked her sweater front to **SL**. It's time to start her short rows! She works to 2 stitches before the end of her row. She does her Wrap & Turn as described above. Now she's got the wrong side of her work facing her. She works to 2 stitches before the end of this row and masterfully performs another W&T. She has worked 1 pair of short rows!

The rest of her W&T adventure goes like this:
For the second pair of short rows she wraps and turns at the 4th stitch from each end, then the third pair on the 6th stitch from each end, then on the 8th, 10th, 12th, 14th, 16th, 18th, 20th, 22nd and 24th stitches from each end. And she's done wrapping!

Step 7: Making the bumps disappear
She's all done making her short rows. She's got the right side of her work facing her; it's time to work to the end of the row, then resume working regular full-length rows again. Every time she comes across a bump (the wrappy part of the Wrap & Turn) she'll pick up the wrap [it's the horizontal bar snugged around the base of the vertical stitch], place it on the left needle, and knit [or purl] it together with the stitch it had previously wrapped. When she works the next row, she'll do the same thing for the remaining wraps. Poof – no gap!

Here's how this last part looks in the chart:

Bust Dart Depth: **FL–BL**	**BDD**	4"
Bust Dart Rows: **BDD** x **R**	**BDR**	24
Front Sweater Width: **SB** ÷ 2	**FSW**	24"
Bust Dart Width: **(FSW – TND)** ÷ 2	**BDW**	6"
Bust Dart Stitches: **BDW** x **S**	**BDS**	24
Turning Points for each side: **BDR** ÷ 2	**TP**	12
Short Row Increments: **BDS** ÷ **TP**	**SRI**	2

It's not scary when you work it step by step. So work it!

Stop and Read This Very Important Thing:

When our math says, "The short rows will be worked in 2 stitch increments," this does NOT mean that there will be 2 unwrapped stitches between each W&T. Remember, each time you wrap and turn, that wrap takes up 1 stitch which counts as 1 of the 2. So when you work your first short row, which ends 2 stitches before the end of the row, you will wrap the second-last stitch in the row (A). The next time you wrap and turn on that side of the sweater, you will wrap the fourth-last stitch of the row (B); there will only be 1 stitch (the third-last stitch) between wraps (C).

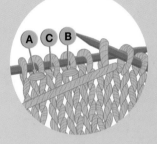

Here's a complete chart for you to use! Photocopy it and fill it in for any sweater you want to modify.

What is it?	Secret code	My numbers
Body Stuff		
Front Length (shoulder to front waist, over your boobs)	FL	
Back Length (shoulder to back waist)	BL	
Front/Back Difference: **FL − BL**	FBD	
Side length (hem to bottom of bra band - 1" or 2" below armhole)	SL	
Nipple Distance (horizontal distance between nipples)	ND	
Tasteful Nipple Distance (so short rows don't peak on your nipples): **ND + 2"**	TND	
Sweater Stuff		
Stitch gauge per inch	S	
Row gauge per inch	R	
Sweater Bust	SB	
Bust Dart Depth: **FL − BL**	BDD	
Bust Dart Rows: **BDD x R**	BDR	
Front Sweater Width: **SB ÷ 2**	FSW	
Bust Dart Width: **(FSW − TND) ÷ 2**	BDW	
Bust Dart Stitches: **BDW x S**	BDS	
Turning Points for each side: **BDR ÷ 2**	TP	
Short Row Increments: **BDR ÷ TP**	SRI	

LEVELS OF DIFFICULTY

Each of the patterns in this book is rated according to how much concentration it requires. Just look for these numbers next to the B3 icons, and select a project that's right for you.

(1) half-caf (brain nudge)
straightforward knitting with shaping

(2) espresso (modest amount of brain fuel)
shaping, color work, multiple stitch patterns

(3) triple-shot caffeine bomb with whipped cream (all brain cells on full)
complex shaping with multiple things happening at the same time

chapter 5

Pullovers

Stacy Pullover

Sexy Ribs Pullover

Amelia Corset

Whichway Funnelneck

Mosaic Sweater

SIZE
L[1X, 2X, 3X]

FINISHED MEASUREMENTS
[in inches]
Chest: 40[44, 48, 52]
Length: 21[21, 22, 22]

MATERIALS
Tahki Stacy Charles New Tweed
[70% merino wool, 15% silk,
11% cotton, 4% viscose; 103
yds/95 m per 50g skein]; color:
034; 11[12, 14, 16] skeins

1 set US #8/5mm needles

1 set US #6/4mm needles

Cable needle

Stitch holder

Tapestry needle

4.5 mm crochet hook

GAUGE
24 sts/28 rows = 4 inches in
2 x 3 Rib using smaller needles

24 sts/32 rows = 4 inches in
Slipped Honeycomb stitch using
larger needles

Stacy Pullover

by Terri Shea

THIS SWEATER HAS AN INTERESTING ALL-OVER PATTERN and a body-skimming fit that smoothes curves. The ribbing builds in a waist and the V neck is just the ticket for boob flattery. Don't be tempted to knit it larger than your body measurements…you'll just be knitting extra fabric that will hang there limply wondering "why did you create me if I serve no purpose?" Knit it to fit. This is one close-fitting sweater that wants to show off everything you've got in the best way it knows how. We like a sweater with good intentions.

Pattern

BACK

Rib

*Using smaller needles, CO 87[97, 102, 112] sts. *[see Fitting Tip in Pattern Notes]* Work in 2 x 3 Rib until work measures 6 inches, ending with a RS row.

Body

Row 1: [WS]: [P2, k1, kfb, k1] to last 2 sts, p2. 104[116, 122, 134] sts.
Rows 2–5: Using larger needles, work in Slipped Honeycomb stitch (see page 34). *Work new sts in reverse St st until 3 sts have been increased on each side, then incorporate these sts into patt.*

Row 6 [RS]: K1, m1, work in patt as set to last st, m1, k1.
Rows 7–9: Work in patt as set.
Repeat *Rows 6–9* 8[9, 11, 11] times more. 122[136, 146, 158] sts.

Cont in patt as set until work measures 12.5[12.5, 13.5, 13.5] inches, ending with a WS row.

Shape armholes

BO 6[10, 12, 16] sts at beg of next 2 rows.
BO 3 sts at beg of foll 2 rows.
BO 2 sts at beg of foll 2 rows.

Row 7 [RS]: K1, k2tog, work in patt as set to last 3 sts, ssk, k1.
Row 8: Work in patt as set.
Repeat *Rows 7 and 8* 6[6, 6, 8] times more. 86[92, 98, 98] sts rem.*

Cont in patt as set until work measures 20.5[20.5, 21.5, 21.5] inches, ending with a WS row.

Shape shoulders and neckline

Left and right shoulders and neckline are divided and worked separately.

Pattern Notes

FITTING TIP: If you have a pear-shaped figure, you may wish to use larger needles than specified for casting on and working rib; or, using needles suggested, CO 104[116, 122, 134] sts and work in 2 x 4 Rib instead of 2 x 3 Rib. If you choose this second option, DO NOT work increase row at end of rib section, and end rib on a WS row instead of on a RS row as written.
If you have a very small waist, you may wish to use even smaller needles than US #6/4mm for the rib, such as US #4/3.5mm.

2 X 3 Rib: (Worked over a multiple of 5 sts + 2)
Row 1 [RS]: [K2, p3] to last 2 sts, k2.
Row 2 [WS]: [P2, k3] to last 2 sts, p2.
Repeat these 2 rows for 2x3 rib. >>

C3B: Slip next 2 sts to cable needle and hold to back of work, k1, p2 from cable needle.

C3F: Slip next st to cable needle, hold to front of work, p2, k1 from cable needle.

SLIPPED HONEYCOMB STITCH: (Worked over a multiple of 6 sts + 2):
Note: Slip all slipped sts purlwise with yarn held to WS of work.
Row 1 [RS]: K1, [C3F, C3B] to last st, k1.
Row 2 [WS]: P1, k2, p2, [k4, p2] to last 3 sts, k2, p1.
Row 3 [RS]: K1, p2, [sl2, p4] to last 5 sts, sl2, p2, k1.
Row 4 [WS]: P1, k2, [sl2, k4] to last 5 sts, sl2, k2, p1.
Row 5 [RS]: K1, [C3B, C3F] to last st, k1.
Row 6 [WS]: P2, [k4, p2] to end.
Row 7 [RS]: K1, sl1, [p4, sl2] to last 6 sts, p4, sl1, k1.
Row 8 [WS]: P1, sl1, [k4, sl2] to last 6 sts, k4, sl1, p1.

Left shoulder and neckline
Row 1: [RS]: BO 8[9, 9, 9] sts, work next 15[17, 18, 18] sts in patt (16 [18, 19, 19] sts on right needle), place rem sts on holder for right shoulder and neckline.
Row 2: Work in patt as set.
Row 3 [RS]: BO 8[9, 9, 9] sts, work in patt to last 3 sts, ssk, k1.
Row 4: Work in patt as set.
Row 5 [RS]: BO rem 7[8, 9, 9] sts.

Right shoulder and neckline
Place held sts on needle with RS facing, and rejoin yarn.
Row 6: BO 38[38, 42, 42] center sts, work in patt as set to end.
Row 7 [WS]: BO 8[9, 9, 9] sts, work in patt as set to end.
Row 8: Work in patt as set.
Row 9 [WS]: BO 8[9, 9, 9] sts, work in patt as set to last 3 sts, p2tog, p1.
Row 10: Work in patt as set.
Row 11 [WS]: BO rem 7[8, 9, 9] sts.

FRONT
Work as for Back from * to * through Armhole Shaping.
Cont in patt as set until work measures 15[15.5, 16, 16] inches, ending with a WS row.

Shape shoulders and neckline
Left and right shoulders and neckline are divided and worked seperately.

Left shoulder and neckline
Row 1 [RS]: Work 41[44, 47, 47] sts in patt as set, k2tog, place rem sts on holder. For neck and right shoulder. Work in patt as set until work measures 18[18, 19, 19] inches, ending with a RS Row.

Row 2 [WS]: BO 7 sts, work to end in patt as set.
Row 3: Work in patt as set.
Row 4: BO 3 sts, work to end in patt as set.
Row 5: Work in patt as set.
Row 6 [WS]: BO 2 sts, work to end in patt as set.

Row 7 [RS]: Work in patt as set to last 2 sts, k2tog.
Row 8: Work in patt as set.
Repeat *Rows 7 and 8* 7[6, 8, 8] times more.
AT THE SAME TIME: When work measures 20.5[20.5, 21.5, 21.5] inches, ending with a WS row, bind off sts for shoulder as foll:

Left shoulder bind off
Row 1 [RS]: BO 8[9, 9, 9] sts, work to end in patt as set.
Row 2: Work in patt as set.
Row 3 [RS]: BO 8[9, 9, 9] sts, work work to end in patt as set.
Row 4: Work in patt as set.
Row 5 [RS]: BO rem 7[8, 9, 9] sts.

Right shoulder and neckline
Place held sts on needle with RS facing, and rejoin yarn.
Ssk, work to end in patt as set.
Work in patt as set until work measures 18[18, 19, 19] inches, ending with a WS Row.

Row 1 [RS]: BO 7 sts, work to end in patt as set.
Row 2: Work in patt as set.
Row 3 [RS]: BO 3 sts, work to end in patt as set.
Row 4: Work patt as set.
Row 5 [RS]: BO 2 sts, work to end in patt as set.
Row 6: Work in patt as set.
Row 7 [RS]: Ssk, work in patt as set to end.
Row 8: Work in patt as set.
Repeat *Rows 7 and 8* 7[6, 8, 8] times more.
AT THE SAME TIME: When work measures 20.5[20.5, 21.5, 21.5] inches, ending with a WS row, bind off sts for shoulder as foll:

Right shoulder bind off
Row 1 [WS]: BO 8[9, 9, 9] sts, work to end in patt as set.
Row 2: Work in patt as set.
Row 3 [WS]: BO 8[9, 9, 9] sts, work work to end in patt as set.
Row 4: Work in patt as set.
Row 5 [WS]: BO rem 7[8, 9, 9] sts.

SLEEVES (MAKE 2)

Using smaller needles, CO 42(42, 52, 52) sts.

Work 4 rows in 2x3 Rib.

Row 1 [RS]: K1, m1, work in patt as set to last st, m1, k1.

Rows 2–4: Work in patt as set, keeping edge sts in St st.

Repeat *Rows 1–4* 19[23, 22, 28] times more, incorporating new sts into rib patt, keeping edge sts in St st. 82[90, 98, 110] sts.

Incorporate new sts into rib pattern while keeping edge sts in stockinette

Work in patt as set until work measures 17.5 inches, or desired length.

Shape sleeve cap

BO 6[10, 12, 16] sts at beg of next 2 rows.

BO 3 sts at beg of foll 2 rows.

BO 2 sts at beg of foll 2 rows. 60[60, 64, 68] sts rem.

Rows 1 and 2: Work in patt as set.

Row 3 [RS]: K1, k2tog, work in patt as set to last 3 sts, ssk, k1.

Rows 4 and 5: Work in patt as set.

Row 6 [WS]: P1, p2tog tbl, work in patt as set to last 3 sts, p2tog, p1.

Repeat these 6 rows 5[5, 6, 6] times more. 36[36, 36, 40] sts rem.

BO 6 sts at beg of next 2 rows.

BO rem 24[24, 24, 28] sts.

Finishing

Block all pieces lightly.

Sew back to front at shoulder seams.

Sew sleeve caps into armholes.

Sew sleeve seams and side seams.

Using crochet hook, work 1 row of single crochet around neckline.

Weave in all ends.

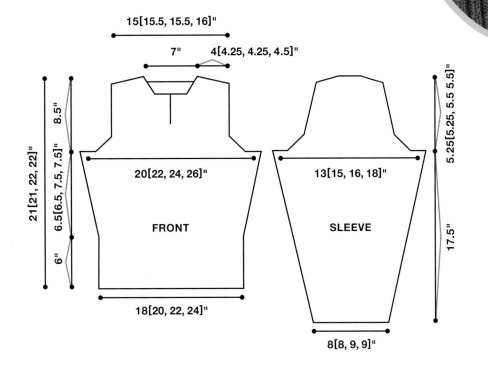

15[15.5, 15.5, 16]"

7" 4[4.25, 4.25, 4.5]"

8.5"

21[21, 22, 22]"

6.5[6.5, 7.5, 7.5]"

6"

20[22, 24, 26]"

FRONT

18[20, 22, 24]"

5.25[5.25, 5.5 5.5]"

13[15, 16, 18]"

SLEEVE

17.5"

8[8, 9, 9]"

SIZE
L[1X, 2X, 3X, 4X, 5X]

FINISHED MEASUREMENTS
[in inches]
Bust: Varies from 1 inch to 6 inches larger than under-bust circumference, depending on cup size.
Under-bust: 40.75[43.75, 50, 53.25, 59.5, 62.5]
Hip: 47[50, 56.25, 59.5, 65.75, 68.75]
Length: 26[26.25, 26.75, 27.25, 28, 28.5]

To select size, start with your under-bust measurement (chest circumference measured below bust, around lower edge of bra band); choose a size with an under-bust measurement that is 5% larger than your actual measurement. The pattern is customized for different bust sizes when working bust section of pattern.

MATERIALS
Cascade Yarns Indulgence [70% alpaca, 30% angora; 123 yds/110 m per 50g ball]; color: 521 Lavender; 15[16, 18, 19, 22, 23] balls for hourglass shape; add 1 ball for pear, straight, or apple shape

1 29-inch US #5/3.75mm circular needle

1 16-inch US #5/3.75mm circular needle

1 set US #5/3.75mm double-pointed needles

Stitch markers

Stitch holders

Tapestry needle

GAUGE
20 sts/24 rows = 4 inches in St stitch

23 sts/22 rows = 4 inches in Wavy Rib pattern

Sexy Ribs Pullover

by Kate Kuckro

LIKE WE'VE SAID, there's a difference between sausage casing and curve hugging. This sweater is all about embracing your curves. The lace is designed vertically, but it never sits still. It waves and your eyes follow. The unique and revealing bodice is designed to flatter all sizes of boobage. Our advice: wear a great push-up bra and keep your business cards handy.

Pattern

LOWER BODY

Using longer circular needle, CO 240[256, 288, 304, 336, 352] sts. Place marker and join to begin working in the round, being careful not to twist.
Round 1: [P2, k2] around.
Work in 2 x 2 Rib as set until work measures 3 inches.

Next Round: Work 120[128, 144, 152, 168, 176] sts in 2 x 2 Rib, place marker to mark side "seam" placement, cont to end in patt.

Beg at point indicated for your size, work the 6 setup rounds of Chart A(S1 to S6). 270[288, 324, 342, 378, 396] sts.

Shape waist: customize based on waist and hip measurements

Subtract your waist circumference from your hip circumference, and choose the shaping option that best suits you (see below).

Begin working all charts from Row 1 unless otherwise specified.

For sizes L, 3X, and 4X only: *When the directions call for half of a repeat of Chart A, continue working the pattern as established in set-up rounds (i.e. beg at the 6th stitch, end at 5th stitch of Chart A).*

Hourglass
(waist is 8 to 14 inches smaller)
Work 12 rounds of Chart A.

Next Round: [Work 0.5[1, 1, 1.5, 2.5, 2] repeats of Chart A, 1 repeat of Chart B, 1[1, 2, 2, 2, 3] repeats of Chart A, 1 repeat of Chart B, 4 repeats of Chart A, 1 repeat of Chart B, 1[1, 2, 2, 2, 3] repeats of Chart A, 1 repeat of Chart B, and 0.5[1, 1, 1.5, 2.5, 2] repeats of Chart A] twice.
Work 6 more rounds in patt, working through all rows of Chart B as set.

Work increases as specified in Chart C or in the patt directions, as follows. M1: with left needle, lift strand between needles from front to back; knit into back of lifted loop, or MP1: with left needle, lift strand between needles from back to front; purl lifted loop.

Use stitch markers to mark changes from one chart to another as needed.

If you plan to customize the pattern beyond the options provided below, please note that for every 8 sts decreased (or increased), in Wavy Rib you've actually lost (or gained) an extra ninth stitch due to the drop stitch pattern.

W2TOG: Work 2 sts tog in patt. (If the next st is a p st, p2tog. If it is a k st, k2tog.)
W2TOG TBL: Work 2 sts tog through back loops.

Work Chart A for 11 rounds, beg with row 8 and ending with row 6.

Next Round: [Work 1.5[2, 2, 2.5, 3.5, 3] repeats of Chart A, 1 repeat of Chart C, 6[6, 8, 8, 8, 10] repeats of Chart A, 1 repeat of Chart C, and 1.5[2, 2, 2.5, 3.5, 3] repeats of Chart A] twice. Work 6 more rounds in patt, working through all rows of Chart C as set.

Proceed to **"Continue here."**

Pear (waist is 3 to 8 inches smaller)
Work 12 rounds of Chart A.

Next Round: [Work 2.5[2, 3, 3.5, 3.5, 4] repeats of Chart A, 1 repeat of chart B, 6[6, 8, 8, 8, 10] repeats of Chart A, 1 repeat of Chart B, and 2.5[2, 3, 3.5, 3.5, 4] repeats of Chart A] twice.

Work 6 more rounds in patt, working through all rows of Chart B as set.

Work Chart A for 18 rounds, beg with Row 8 and ending with Row 1.

Proceed to **"Continue here."**

Straight (waist is 3 inches smaller to 3 inches larger)
Work 24 rounds of Chart A.

Next Round: [Work 2.5[2, 3, 3.5, 3.5, 4] repeats of Chart A, 1 repeat of chart B, 6[6, 8, 8, 8, 10] repeats of Chart A, 1 repeat of Chart B, and 2.5[2, 3, 3.5, 3.5, 4] repeats of Chart A] twice.

Work 6 more rounds in patt, working through all rows of Chart B as set.

Work Chart A for 6 rounds, beg with Row 8 and ending with Row 1.

Proceed to **"Continue here."**

Apple (waist is 4 to 8 inches larger)
Work first 6 rounds of Chart A.

Next Round: [Work 2.5[3, 3, 3.5, 4.5, 4] repeats of Chart A, 1 repeat of Chart C, 8[8, 10, 10, 10, 12] repeats of Chart A, 1 repeat of Chart C, and 2.5[3, 3, 3.5, 4.5, 4] repeats of Chart A] twice.

Work 6 more rounds in patt, working through all rows of Chart C as set.

Work Chart A for 11 rounds, beg with row 2 and ending with row 12.

Next Round: [Work 0.5[1, 2, 1.5, 2.5, 3] repeats of Chart A, 1 repeat of Chart B, 2[2, 2, 3, 3, 3] repeats of Chart A, 1 repeat of Chart B, 4 repeats of Chart A, 1 repeat of Chart B, 2[2, 2, 3, 3, 3] repeats of Chart A, 1 repeat of Chart B, and 0.5[1, 2, 1.5, 2.5, 3] repeats of Chart A] twice.

Work 6 more rounds in patt, working through all rows of Chart B as set.

Work Chart A for 6 rounds, beg with Row 8 and ending with Row 1.

Proceed to **"Continue here."**

Continue here
Work 4[5, 6, 8, 10, 11] rounds of Chart A as established, beg with Row 2. 234[252, 288, 306, 342, 360] sts; work measures 11.5[11.75, 12, 12.25, 12.5, 12.75] inches.

Shape under-bust: customize based on difference between bust and under-bust measurements
Measure your chest beneath your bust (around the bottom of your bra band); this is your under-bust measurement. Measure your chest around the fullest part of your bust, then subtract your under-bust measurement from your full bust measurement. This difference will indicate your approximate cup size for the purposes of this pattern.

Very Important: *When bracketed set of numbers are in bold type, they refer to cup sizes **A[B, C, D, DD, DDD]**; that is, the* *bust measurement is 1[2, 3, 4, 5, 6] inches larger than the under-bust measurement. Both sets of sizes will be used (sweater sizes and bust sizes), be sure you are referring to the correct numbers!*

Work **19[16, 13, 11, 10, 8]** rounds of Chart A as established, or to desired length from lower edge to under-bust.

Divide for Front and Back
Place first 50[54, 63, 68, 77, 81] sts of next round on a st holder, place next 18 sts on short circular needle, place next 50[54, 63, 68, 77, 81] sts on stitch holder. 116[126, 144, 152, 170, 180] sts rem.

UPPER BACK
Work back and forth in patt as set (working from Chart A) on rem sts until work measures 15.5[15.75, 16, 16.25, 16.75, 17] inches, ending with a WS row.
Be sure to read second note under "Pattern Notes" before beginning armhole shaping!

Shape armhole
BO 5[7, 8, 9, 10, 10] sts at beg of next two rows.

BO 4[4, 6, 6, 6, 6] sts at beg of foll two rows.

Next Row [RS]: K1, w2tog, work in patt to last 3 sts, w2tog tbl, k1.
Work 1 row in patt as set.
Repeat these 2 rows 1[1, 2, 3, 4, 4] times more. 92[96, 105, 110, 123, 132] sts rem. *Do not worry if your st count is only 1 or 2 sts off; this may happen as a result of where you are in the st pattern.*

Cont in patt as set until armhole measures 8.25[8.25, 8.5, 8.75, 9, 9.25] inches, ending with a WS row.

Work 4 rows in 2 x 2 Rib
See third note under "Pattern Notes" about making the transition from Wavy Rib pattern to 2 x 2 Rib.

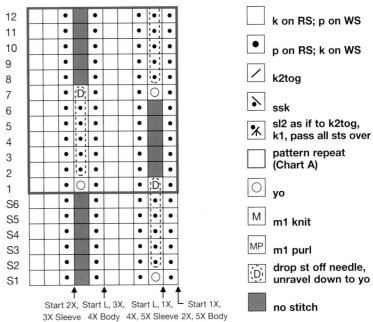

CHART A (WAVY RIB PATTERN)

KEY

☐	k on RS; p on WS
•	p on RS; k on WS
╱	k2tog
╲	ssk
⋇	sl2 as if to k2tog, k1, pass all sts over
☐	pattern repeat (Chart A)
○	yo
M	m1 knit
MP	m1 purl
D	drop st off needle, unravel down to yo
▧	no stitch

Start 2X, 3X Sleeve   Start L, 3X 4X Body   Start L, 1X 4X, 5X Sleeve   Start 1X 2X, 5X Body

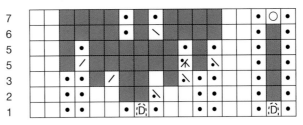

CHART B (WAVY RIB DECREASE)

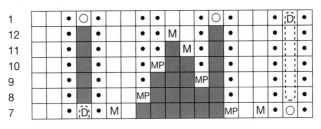

CHART C (WAVY RIB INCREASE)

Next Row [RS]: Work 24[24, 24, 24, 36, 36] sts in patt, place sts just worked on st holder, BO in 2 x 2 Rib until 24[24, 24, 24, 36, 36] sts rem, including working st.
Work 6 rows in patt as set.

Next Row [WS]: BO 8[8, 8, 8, 12, 12] sts, work in patt to end.
Next Row [RS]: Work all sts in patt.
Repeat these 2 rows once more.
BO rem sts.

Replace held sts from right shoulder on needle with RS facing, rejoin yarn. Work 6 rows in patt as set.

Next Row [RS]: BO 8[8, 8, 8, 12, 12] sts, work in patt to end.
Next Row [WS]: Work all sts in patt.
Repeat these 2 rows once more.
BO rem sts.

UPPER FRONT
Shape center point
With RS facing, rejoin yarn to center sts of front held on circular needle.
Next Row [RS]: K1, w2tog, work in 2 x 2 Rib to last 3 sts, w2tog tbl, k1.
Next Row [WS]: Work all sts in patt as set.
Repeat these 2 rows until 4 sts rem.

Next Row [RS]: Ssk, k2tog. Break yarn, draw through rem 2 sts, pull tight.

Very Important: *When bracketed set of numbers are in bold type, they refer to cup sizes **A[B, C, D, DD, DDD]**; that is, the bust measurement is 1[2, 3, 4, 5, 6] inches larger than the underbust measurement. Both sets of sizes will be used (sweater sizes and bust sizes), be sure you are referring to the correct numbers!*

LEFT FRONT
When stitch pattern switches from Wavy Rib pattern (Chart A) to 2 x 2 Rib, line up patterns as follows: maintain 2-st columns of k sts as set, maintain 2-st columns of p sts as set, drop center st of each 3-st column of p sts and work these columns with 2 p sts.

Shape cup
Place sts for Left Front on needle with RS facing, rejoin yarn. (Remember, when the front of the sweater is facing you, the Left Front will be on your right.)
Work 1 row in 2 x 2 Rib.
Next Row [WS]: BO **3[6, 7, 14, 20, 28]** sts (next to center point), work to end in patt.
Work **10[14, 20, 24, 28, 30]** rows in patt, ending with a WS row.

Next Row [RS]: Work all sts in patt, pick up and k **13[17, 22, 26, 30, 33]** sts along edge of section just worked (to edge of BO sts).
Work **20[22, 22, 28, 36, 44]** rows in 2 x 2 Rib over all sts, ending with a RS row. *Edge of section just worked should be long enough to reach along BO sts and edge of center section, to center point.*
AT THE SAME TIME: When work measures same as Back to underarm, ending with a WS row, shape underarm as follows:
Row 1 [RS]: BO 5[7, 8, 9, 10, 10] sts, work to end in patt.
Row 2: Work in patt as set.
Row 3 [RS]: BO 4[4, 6, 6, 6, 6] sts, work to end in patt.
Row 4: Work in patt as set.

Row 5 [RS]: K1, w2tog, work to end in patt.
Row 6: Work in patt as set.
Repeat *Rows 5 and 6* 1[1, 2, 3, 4, 4] times more.

After all rows of cup are complete, proceed as follows:
Next Row [WS]: BO in 2x2 Rib until 26[26, 26, 26, 38, 38] sts rem, work to end in patt.
Work 1 row in patt as set.

Next Row [WS]: W2tog, work to end in patt.

Work 1 row in patt as set.
Repeat these 2 rows once more.

Cont in patt until work measures same as Back to shoulder, ending with a WS row.

Next Row [RS]: BO 8[8, 8, 8, 12, 12] sts, work in patt to end.
Next Row [WS]: Work all sts in patt.
Repeat these 2 rows once more. BO rem sts.

RIGHT FRONT

Read through pattern carefully before continuing, different sets of shaping are worked simultaneously.

Shape cup

Place sts for Right Front on needle with WS facing, rejoin yarn.
Work 1 row in 2 x 2 Rib.
Next Row [RS]: BO **3[6, 7, 14, 20, 28]** sts (next to center point), work to end in patt.
Work **10[14, 20, 24, 28, 30]** rows in patt, ending with a RS row.

Next Row [WS]: Work all sts in patt, pick up and p **13[17, 22, 26, 30, 33]** sts along edge of section just worked (to edge of BO sts).
Work **20[22, 22, 28, 36, 44]** rows in 2x2 Rib over all sts, ending with a WS row. *Edge of section just worked should be long enough to reach along BO sts and edge of center section, to center point.*
AT THE SAME TIME: When work measures same as Back to underarm, ending with a RS row, shape underarm as follows:
Row 1 [WS]: BO 5[7, 8, 9, 10, 10] sts, work to end in patt.
Row 2: Work in patt as set.
Row 3 [WS]: BO 4[4, 6, 6, 6, 6] sts, work to end in patt.

Row 4 [RS]: Work in patt to last 3 sts, w2tog tbl, k1.
Row 5: Work in patt as set.
Repeat *Rows 4 and 5* 1[1, 2, 3, 4, 4] times more.

After all rows of cup are complete, proceed as follows:
Next Row [RS]: BO in 2x2 Rib until 26[26, 26, 26, 38, 38] sts rem, work to end in patt.
Work 1 row in patt as set.

Next row [RS]: W2tog tbl, work to end in patt.
Work 1 row in patt as set.
Repeat these 2 rows once more.

Cont in patt until work measures same as Back to shoulder, ending with a RS row.

Next Row [WS]: BO 8[8, 8, 8, 12, 12] sts, work in patt to end.
Next Row [RS]: Work all sts in patt.
Repeat these 2 rows once more.
BO rem sts.

SLEEVES (MAKE 2)

Using double-pointed needles (or 2 circulars if desired), CO 48[48, 52, 52, 56, 56] sts. Distribute sts evenly among needles and join to begin working in the round, being careful not to twist.

Round 1: K1, place marker, [p2, k2] to last 3 sts, p2, place marker, k1.

1. UNDERBUST HEIGHTS
The underbust heights vary to allow for different starting heights for cups. Select heights based on the difference between your Bust and Underbust Measurements as follows (all measurements are in inches):

DIFFERENCE
1 inch (A cup)
2 inches (B cup)
3 inches (C cup)
4 inches (D cup)
5 inches (DD cup)
6 inches (DDD cup)

2. WAIST MEASUREMENTS
Choose the best waist shape for your body type: Hourglass, Pear, Straight, or Apple (all measurements are in inches):

SHAPE	HIP–WAIST	FINISHED WIDTH
Hourglass	8 to 14	17.2[18.8, 21.9, 23.5, 26.6, 28.2]
Pear	3 to 8	20.3[21.9, 25, 26.6, 29.7, 31.3]
Straight	-3 to 3	23.5[25, 28.2, 29.7, 32.9, 34.4]
Apple	-4 to -8	26.6[28.2, 31.3, 32.9, 36, 37.6]

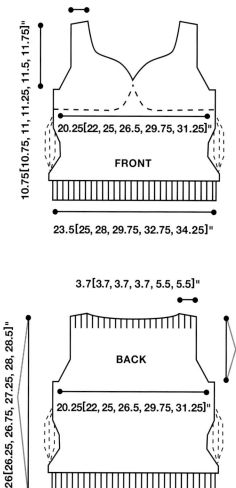

FRONT

3.7[3.7, 3.7, 3.7, 5.5, 5.5]"

10.75[10.75, 11, 11.25, 11.5, 11.75]"

20.25[22, 25, 26.5, 29.75, 31.25]"

23.5[25, 28, 29.75, 32.75, 34.25]"

BACK

3.7[3.7, 3.7, 3.7, 5.5, 5.5]"

26[26.25, 26.75, 27.25, 28, 28.5]"

10.75[10.75, 11, 11.25, 11.5, 11.75]"

20.25[22, 25, 26.5, 29.75, 31.25]"

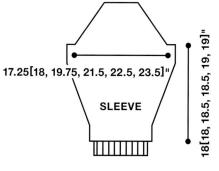

SLEEVE

17.25[18, 19.75, 21.5, 22.5, 23.5]"

18[18, 18.5, 18.5, 19, 19]"

The solid line indicates the shape of the waist worked with Hourglass shaping. Dotted lines show Pear, Straight, and Apple shaping

The 2 sts between markers will be designated the "seam sts," and will always be worked in St st.

Work 14 more rounds in 2 x 2 Rib as set.

Beg at point indicated for your size, work the 6 setup rounds of Chart A (S1 to S6).
Read fourth note under "Pattern Notes" about working increases in pattern; switch to shorter circular needle when there are enough sts on needle.

Sizes 2X, 3X, 4X, 5X only:
Increase Round: K1, slip marker, inc 1, work in patt as set to marker, inc 1, slip marker, k1.
Work 1 round in patt as set.
Repeat these 2 rounds –[–, 4, 14, 15, 17] times more. –[–, 69, 91, 99, 103] sts.

All sizes:
Work *Increase Round* as above.
Work 2 rounds in patt as set.
Repeat these 3 rounds 19[21, 19, 13, 13, 13] times more. 99[103, 114, 123, 130, 135] sts.

Cont in patt as set until sleeve measures 18[18, 18.5, 18.5, 19, 19] inches, or desired length to underarm.

Next Round: Work in patt to 4[6, 7, 8, 9, 9] sts before second marker; BO 9[13, 16, 17, 20, 19] sts.

Work 1 row in patt as set; Sleeve Cap will now be worked back and forth.
BO 4[4, 6, 6, 6, 6] sts at beg of next two rows.
Work 1 row in patt as set.

Decrease Row [RS]: K1, w2tog, work to last 3 sts, w2tog tbl, k1.
Work 1 row in patt as set.
Repeat these 2 rows 1[1, 2, 3, 4, 4] times more. 75[74, 75, 81, 82, 88] sts rem.

Work 2 rows in patt as set.
Work *Decrease Row* as above.
Work 1 row in patt as set.
Repeat these 4 rows 4[4, 4, 2, 3, 2] times more. 66[66, 68, 79, 79, 87] sts rem.

Sizes L, 1X, 3X, 4X, 5X only:
Work *Decrease Row* as above.
Work 1 row in patt as set.
Repeat these 2 rows 1[1, —, 3, 0, 2] times more.

Size 2X only:
Work 2 rows in patt as set.

All sizes:
61[61, 68, 70, 76, 80] sts rem.
BO 3 sts at beg of next 2 rows.
Repeat these 2 rows 0[0, 1, 0, 2, 4] times more. 54[54, 54, 63, 55, 46] sts rem.

BO 4 sts at beg of next 2 rows.
Repeat these 2 rows 3[3, 3, 4, 3, 2] times more.
BO rem sts loosely.

Finishing

Lightly steam press pieces, gently pulling fabric so that the wavy ribs are slightly separated but not fully stretched. Be careful not to press ribbing directly. Sew shoulder seams. Sew sleeves into armholes. Sew edges of cups to adjacent BO sts and edges of center point, overlapping the cups slightly at the center if needed. Weave in ends.

SIZE
L[1X, 2X, 3X]

FINISHED MEASUREMENTS
[in inches]
Chest: 44[48, 52, 56]
Waist: 35[39,43,47]
Length: 24[24, 25, 25]

MATERIALS
[MC] Colinette Giotto [50%
cotton, 40% rayon, 10% nylon;
156 yds/140 m per 100g skein];
color: 127 Morocco; 4[5, 6, 6]
skeins

[CC] Rowan Calmer [75%
cotton, 25% microfiber;
178 yds/160 m per 50g skein];
color: 475 Tinkerbell; 2[3, 4, 4]
skeins

1 set US #6/4mm needles

1 set US #10/6mm needles

1 16-inch US #10/6mm
circular needle

Stitch markers

Safety pin

Stitch holder

Tapestry needle

GAUGE
16 sts/20 rows =
4 inches in St stitch using MC

24 sts/28 rows =
4 inches in St stitch using CC

Amelia Corset

by Jillian Moreno for Acme Knitting Company

THIS CORSET-SHAPED TOP is the perfect way to show off sexy flesh in a socially acceptable way. We love this top cause it lets you work with two of the nicest yarns we've ever met...a shimmery ribbon and a nearly edible cotton/microfiber blend. The smoother yarn on the bottom is a nice counterbalance for the Big Girl–friendly multi-colored ribbon on the top. We like how the flared sleeves balance the upper arm area, too. Balance is good!

Pattern

BACK

*Using smaller needles and CC, CO 106[118, 130, 142] sts.
Work in 1 x 1 Rib until work measures 9[9, 10, 10] inches (or desired length to bottom of ribcage), ending with WS row.

Next Row [RS]: Using larger needles and MC, k4[8, 4, 0], k2tog, [k4[3, 3, 3], k2tog] 16[20, 24, 28] times, k4[8, 4, 0]. 89[97, 105, 113] sts rem.*
Work in St st until work measures 13.5[13.5, 14, 14] inches, or desired length to underarm.

Shape armhole

BO 7[8, 10, 12] sts at beg of next 2 rows. 75[81, 85, 89] sts rem.

Next row [RS]: K1, k2tog, k to last 3 sts, ssk, k1.
Next row [WS]: P all sts.
Repeat these 2 rows 5[7, 9, 11] times more. 63[65, 65, 65] sts rem.

Cont in St st until armhole measures 9.5[9.5, 10, 10] inches.

Shape shoulders

BO 5 sts at beg of next 4 rows.
BO 6 sts at beg of next 2 rows.
BO rem 31[33, 33, 33] sts.

FRONT

Work as for Back from * to *.

Work in St st until work measures 11[11, 11.5, 11.5] inches. Add short-rowed bust darts at this point if desired; see Chapter 4 for instructions on calculating and working these darts.

Cont in St st until work measures same as back to underarm when measured along outside edge.

Shape armhole

BO 7[8, 10, 12] sts at beg of next 2 rows. 75[81, 85, 89] sts rem.

Pattern Notes

1X1 RIB (Worked over an even number of sts):
Row 1: [K1, p1] to end.
Every row is the same.

SEED STITCH (Worked over an even number of sts):
Row 1 [RS]: [K1, p1] to end.
Row 2 [WS]: [P1, k1] to end.
Repeat these 2 rows for Seed Stitch.

TAME THE RIBBON: Ribbon yarns don't stay neatly in balls. To keep knitting smoothly and keep the yarn from tangling use a zip-top bag. Poke a small hole in the bottom of the bag, thread the yarn end through the hole, and seal the naughty ball of ribbon in the bag.

To keep variegated yarn colors from pooling into clumps, alternate between two balls of yarn every two rows.

LEFT FRONT AND NECKLINE

Row 1 [RS]: K1, k2tog, k 31[34, 36, 38], ssk, k1, place next st on safety pin, place rem 37[40, 42, 44] sts on st holder.
Row 2 [WS]: P to end.

Row 3 [RS]: K1, k2tog, k to last 3 sts, ssk, k1.
Row 4 [WS]: P all sts.
Repeat *Rows 3 and 4* 4[6, 8, 9] times more. 25[24, 22, 22] sts rem.

Next Row [RS]: K to last 3 sts, ssk, k1.
Work 3 rows in St st.
Repeat these 4 rows 8[7, 5, 5] times more. 16 sts rem.

Cont until work measures same as back to shoulder, ending with a WS row.

Next Row [RS]: BO 5 sts, k to end.
Next Row [WS]: P all sts.
Repeat these 2 rows once more.

BO rem 6 sts.

RIGHT FRONT AND NECKLINE

Replace held sts from Right Front on needle with RS facing, rejoin yarn.
Next Row [RS]: K1, k2tog, k to last 3 sts, ssk, k1.
Next Row [WS]: P all sts.
Repeat these 2 rows 5[7, 9, 10] times more. 25[24, 22, 22] sts rem.

Next Row [RS]: K1, k2tog, k to end.
Work 3 rows in St st.
Repeat these 4 rows 8[7, 5, 5] times more. 16 sts rem.

Cont until work measures same as back to shoulder, ending with a RS row.

Next Row [WS]: BO 5 sts, p to end.
Next Row [RS]: K all sts.
Repeat these 2 rows once more.

BO rem 6 sts.

SLEEVES (MAKE 2)

Using larger needles and MC, CO 44[44,54,54] sts.
Work 2 rows in Seed Stitch.

Next Row [RS]: K1, k2tog, work in patt to last 3 sts, p2tog, k1.
Next Row [WS]: Work all sts in patt as set.
Next Row [RS]: K1, p2tog, work in patt to last 3 sts, k2tog, p1. 40[40, 50, 50] sts rem.
Cont in Seed Stitch until work measures 2.5 inches, ending with a WS row.

Work 4 rows in St st.

Increase Row [RS]: K1, m1, k to last st, m1, k1.
Work 3 rows in St st,
Repeat these 4 rows 17[17, 5, 5] times more. 76[76, 62, 62] sts.

Sizes 2X and 3X only:

Work *Increase Row*.
Work 5 rows in St st.
Repeat these 6 rows –[–, 8, 8] times more. –[–, 80, 80] sts.

All sizes:

Cont in St st until work measures 18.5[18.5, 19.5, 19.5] inches, or desired length to underarm.

BO 7[8, 10, 12] sts at beg of next 2 rows. 62[60, 60, 56] sts rem.

Decrease Row [RS]: K1, k2tog, k to last 2 sts, ssk, k1.
Next row [WS]: P all sts.
Repeat these 2 rows 5[7, 9, 10] times more. 50[44, 40, 34] sts rem.

Work *Decrease Row* as above.
Next Row [WS]: P1, p2tog tbl, p to last 3 sts, p2tog, p1.
Repeat these 2 rows 5[3, 2, 1] times more. 26[28, 28, 26] sts rem.

Sizes L and 1X only:

Work *Decrease Row* once more. P 1 row. 24[26, –, –] sts rem.

All sizes:
BO 3 sts at beg of next 4 rows.
12[14, 16, 14] sts rem.
BO rem sts.

Finishing

Sew shoulder seams.
Sew sleeves into armholes.
Sew sleeve and side seams.

NECKBAND

Using circular needle and MC, with RS
facing and beg at Right shoulder seam,
pick up and k 31[33, 33, 33] back neck
sts, 3 sts in every 4 rows down left front
neckline, k held center front st and use
safety pin to mark this st, pick up and k
3 sts in every 4 rows up right front
neckline. Place marker to indicate beg
of round.

Next Round: Work in Seed Stitch to 1 st
before center front st, work next 3 sts
tog in patt, work to end in Seed Stitch.
Repeat this round 3 times more.

BO all sts loosely.
Weave in ends.

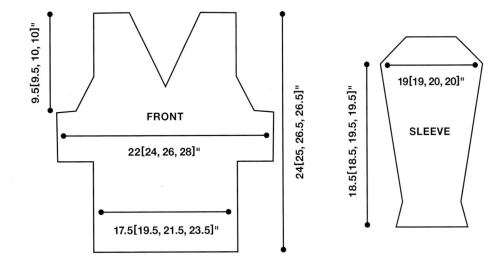

FRONT

22[24, 26, 28]"

17.5[19.5, 21.5, 23.5]"

9.5[9.5, 10, 10]"

24[25, 26.5, 26.5]"

SLEEVE

19[19, 20, 20]"

18.5[18.5, 19.5, 19.5]"

SIZE
L[1X, 2X, 3X]

FINISHED MEASUREMENTS
[in inches]
Chest: 46[50, 54, 58]
Length from Shoulder: 29.5[29.5, 30.5, 31.5]

MATERIALS
Filatura di Crosa, 127 Print [100% wool; 93 yds/85 m per 50g skein]; color: 25; 17[18,19,20] skeins

1 24-inch US #7/4.5mm circular needle

1 16-inch US #7/4.5mm circular needle

1 spare circular needle, any length, US #7/4.5mm or smaller

1 set US #7/4.5mm double-pointed needles

4.5 mm crochet hook

Waste yarn (smooth yarn, such as mercerized cotton, is recommended)

Cable needle

Stitch holders

Tapestry needle

GAUGE
16 sts/18 rows = 4 inches in St stitch

Whichway Funnelneck

by Deb White

YOU HAVE TO WATCH VARIEGATED YARN...it can create sneaky horizontals where you don't want them. But the barely variegated yarn in this sweater is subtle to begin with. Then it's knit side to side, to create verticals instead of horizontals. The horizontal-ish sections are lusciously cabled, which gives way more vertical oomph than a single cable would. The tall funnelneck is feminine and balances a big belly and/or butt as it draws the eye up. And, if you need some extra wiggle room, the pattern includes instructions for short rows at the hip.

Pattern

CENTER FRONT PANEL

Using Crochet Cast On, CO 52[52, 61,61] sts onto longer circular needle.
Rows 1 and 3 [RS]: P1, k1, p3, [k6, p3] 5[5, 6, 6] times, k1, p1.
Rows 2, 4, and 6 [WS]: K1, p1, k3, [p6, k3] 5[5, 6, 6] times, p1, k1.
Row 5 [RS]: P1, k1, p3, [C6F, p3] 5[5, 6, 6] times, k1, p1.
Repeat these 6 rows until work measures 24[24, 25, 26] inches, ending with *Row 6*.

Next Row [RS]: P1, k1, p3, [(k2tog) 3 times, p3] 5[5, 6, 6] times, k1, p1 37 [37, 43, 43] sts.

Right neck shaping

Row 1 [WS]: Work 12 sts in patt as set, place rem 25 [25, 31, 31] sts on st holder.
Row 2 [RS]: BO 3 sts, work in patt as set to end.
Row 3: Work in patt as set.

Row 4 [RS]: BO 2 sts, work in patt as set to end.
Row 5: Work in patt as set.
Repeat *Rows 4 and 5* once more.
5 sts rem.

Row 8 [RS]: K1, k2tog, work in patt as set to end.
Row 9: Work in patt.
Repeat *Rows 8 and 9* twice more.
2 sts rem.

K2tog, break yarn, draw through rem st.

Left neck shaping

Leaving center 13[13, 19, 19] sts on holder, place 12 sts for Left Neck on needle with RS facing.
Row 1 [RS]: Work patt as set on these 12 sts.
Row 2 [WS]: BO 3 sts, work in patt as set to end.
Row 3 [RS]: Work in patt as set.

Pattern Notes

Base the size you knit on your bust measurement, and adjust as you need to.

C6F: Place next 3 sts on cable needle and hold to front of work, k3, k3 from cable needle.

CROCHET CAST ON: Using waste yarn, work a crochet chain several sts longer than the number of sts to be cast on. Starting 1 or 2 sts in from end of chain and using working yarn, pick up and k 1 st in the back loop of each st until the required number of sts have been worked. Later, the chain will be unraveled and the resulting live sts picked up.

Row 4 [WS]: BO 2 sts, work in patt as set to end.
Row 5 [RS]: Work in patt as set.
Repeat *Rows 4 and 5* once more.
8 sts rem.
Row 8 [WS]: P1, p2tog tbl, work in patt as set to end.
Row 9 [RS]*:* Work in patt as set.
Repeat *Rows 8 and 9* twice more.
2 sts rem.

P2tog tbl, break yarn, draw through rem st.

RIGHT FRONT SIDE PANEL

It is not important if you end up with a different number of sts, as long as they are picked up evenly; just be sure you pick up the same number of sts on the other side of the panel when it is time to do so.

Using longer circular needle, CO 14 sts. Continuing from CO sts, with RS facing, starting at top of left-hand side of panel (will be right side of panel when worn), pick up and k 122[122, 125, 128] sts (approx. 3 sts for every 4 rows). 136[136, 139, 142] sts.

Next Row [WS]: [P4, k1] to last 1[1, 4, 2] sts, p to end.
Next Row [RS]: K1[1, 4, 2], [p1, k4] to end.
Repeat these 2 rows until work measures 4[4.5, 4.5, 5] inches from edge of center panel, ending with a RS row.

Optional hip shaping with short rows

Each pair of short rows will add slightly less than half an inch of width to the panel. When you are deciding how many short rows to work, remember that you will be working the same short rows on the other front side panel, as well as both back panels, so add one quarter of the desired width to each panel. Make a note of how many short rows have been worked.

If extra fullness is desired at the hip, work short rows as follows:
Work 4 sts in patt, W&T. Work in patt to end.
Work 9 sts in patt, W&T. Work in patt to end.
Work 14 sts in patt, W&T. Work in patt to end.
Continue to work short rows, working each pair 5 sts longer than the last, until desired fullness is reached.

After desired hip shaping is worked, work 1 WS row.
Next Row [RS]: BO 39[39, 40, 41] sts, work in patt to end.
Work 3[3.5, 4, 4.5] inches more in patt.

Place sts on holder or waste yarn.

LEFT FRONT SIDE PANEL

Using longer needle, with RS facing, starting at bottom of right-hand side of panel (will be left side of panel when worn), pick up and k 122[122, 125, 128] sts (or same number of sts as picked up for Right Front Side Panel), then CO 14 sts at end of row. 136[136, 139, 142] sts.

Next Row [WS]: P1[1, 4, 2], [k1, p4] to end.

Next Row [RS]: [K4, p1] to last 1[1, 4, 2] sts, k to end.
Repeat these 2 rows until work measures 4[4.5, 4.5, 5] inches from edge of center panel, ending with a WS row.

Work hip shaping if desired, to match shaping on Right Front Side Panel. *Short rows on this panel will begin on a RS row.*

After desired hip shaping is worked, work 1 RS row.
Next Row [WS]: BO 39[39, 40, 41] sts, work in patt to end.
Work 3[3.5, 4, 4.5] inches more in patt.

Place sts on st holder or waste yarn.

CENTER BACK PANEL
Using Crochet Cast On, CO 36[36, 42, 42] sts onto longer circular needle.
RS Rows: P1, k1, p3, k to last 5 sts, p3, k1, p1.
WS Rows: K1, p1, k3, p to last 5 sts, k3, p1, k1.
Repeat these 2 rows until work measures 9[9, 10, 10] inches, ending with a WS row.

Next Row [RS]: P1, k1, p3, [K2, p1] to last 4 sts, p2, k1, p1.
Next Row [WS]: K1, p1, k3, [p2, k1] to last 4 sts, k2, p1, k1.
Work 3.5 inches in rib as set.

RS Rows: P1, k1, p3, k to last 5 sts, p3, k1, p1.
WS Rows: K1, p1, k3, p to last 5 sts, k3, p1, k1.
Cont in patt as set until work measures same as front to shoulder.

Place all sts on st holder or waste yarn.

LEFT BACK SIDE PANEL
Using longer circular needle, with RS facing, starting at top of left side of panel, pick up and k 136[136, 139, 142] sts.

You should have the same number of sts as you had for either side front panel (including additional CO sts of side front panels). If you are a few sts off, increase or decrease the necessary number of sts evenly over the next row.

Work as for Right Front Side Panel.

RIGHT BACK SIDE PANEL
Using longer needle, with RS facing, starting at bottom of right side of panel, pick up and k 136[136, 139, 142] sts (or same number of sts as picked up for Left Back Side Panel).

Work as for Left Front Side Panel.

Place held sts from Left Back Side Panel and Left Front Side Panel on needles (place one set of sts on longer needle and other set on spare needle). Starting at the bottom and using a Three-Needle Bind Off, join panels. Stop when there are 6 sts remaining on each panel; do not fasten off your working BO st. Place it on the back needle, transfer the front needle to your other hand, so the RS of the work is facing you. There are 13 sts on the needles.

UNDERARM GUSSET
K 1 st (previously working BO st), turn work.
K2, turn work.
K3, turn work.
Continue working back and forth in garter st, working 1 more st on each short row, until all 13 underarm sts have been worked.
Place these sts on st holder or waste yarn.

Join Right Side Panels and make gusset in the same way.

SLEEVES

When working sleeves, switch to double-pointed needles when necessary.
Sew Right Front and Back Side panels together at shoulder, using mattress st. Using shorter needle, pick up and k 1 st in each bound-off st at armhole (omit sts in seam allowance). 76[76, 78, 80] sts. Work back and forth in St st for 3[3.5, 4, 4.5] inches, ending with a WS row.

Next Row [RS]: K all sts, place marker, k held sts from Gusset, place marker, join to begin working in the round. 89[89, 91, 93] sts.

Switch to knitting in the round.

Gusset decrease

Next Round: K to marker, p2tog, p to 2 sts before next marker, p2tog.
K 1 round.
Repeat these 2 rounds until 3 sts rem in gusset.

SLEEVE

Round 1: K to marker, p2tog, p1.
K 1 round.
Round 2: K to marker, p2tog. 1 st rem between markers.
This st will be referred to as the "seam st" and will mark the end of each round. Maintain this st in garter st; markers may be removed if desired.
Round 3: K 1 round. 77[77, 79, 81] sts rem.
Round 4: K1, ssk, k to 3 sts before seam st, k2tog, k1, work seam st as set.
Work *Rounds 5–7* as set.
Repeat *Rounds 4–7* 14 times more. 47[47, 49, 51] sts rem.

Work until sleeve measures 16.5 inches from underarm, or 2 inches less than desired length.

Sizes L, 1X, 3X only:

Next Round: K to seam st, m1, k1. 48[48, 52, 52] sts.

Size 2X only:

Next Round: K to seam st, k2tog. 48 sts.

All sizes:

Next Round: [K2, p2] around. Seam st is no longer worked.
Repeat this round for 2 inches.

BO all sts loosely.

Make Left Sleeve in the same way.

LOWER FRONT BAND

With RS facing, using longer needle, pick up and k 3 sts for every 4 rows along lower edge of Right Front Side Panel, place marker.
Remove crochet chain from CO edge of Front Panel and place resulting live sts on double-pointed needle; work them onto longer needle as follows: k2tog, [p3, (k2tog) 3 times] to last 5 sts, p3, k2tog, place marker.
Pick up and k 3 sts for every 4 rows along lower edge of Left Front Side Panel.
Row 1 [WS]: K to marker, p1, [k3, p3] to 4 sts before marker, k3, p1, k to end.
Row 2 [RS]: K to marker, k1, [p3, k3] to 4 sts before marker, p3, k1, k to end.
Work *Row 1* once more.

Next Row [RS]: K to marker, k1, [p3, slip 3 sts with yarn in front] to 4 sts before marker, p3, k1, k to end.
Next Row [WS]: K to marker, p1, [k3, slip 3 sts with yarn in back] to 4 sts before marker, k3, p1, k to end.
These 2 rows form decorative strands of yarn wrapped around each k rib on RS of work. When slipping sts, be sure yarn is pulled taut before working next st.

Repeat *Rows 1 and 2* until band measures 3 inches.

BO all sts loosely.

LOWER BACK BAND

With RS facing, using longer needle, pick up and k 3 sts for every 4 rows along lower edge of Left Back Side

Panel, remove crochet chain from CO of Back Panel and k resulting live sts, pick up and k 3 sts for every 4 rows along lower edge of Right Back Side Panel. Work in garter st (k every row) until band measures 3 inches.

BO all sts loosely.
Sew Front Band to Back Band at sides.

COLLAR

Place 36[36, 42, 42] held sts from back neck on shorter circular needle, k these sts, then pick up and k 1 st in each of the 14 CO sts at upper edge of Left Front Side Panel, pick up and k 5 sts along shaped vertical left edge of neckline, pick up and k 1 st in each of the 7 bound-off st of left front neckline, k 13[13, 19, 19] held sts at center front of neckline, pick up and k sts along right edge of neckline to match. 101[101, 111, 111] sts. Place marker (at right shoulder seam) and join to begin working in the round.

Sizes L and 1X only:
K 1 round, increasing 1 st at center front. 102 sts.

Sizes 2X and 3X only:
Next Round: [K35, k2tog] 3 times. 108 sts.

All sizes:
Next Round: [K3, p3] around.
Repeat this round for 4 inches.
BO all sts loosely.

Finishing

Sew upper edges of sleeves to bound-off edges of armholes.
Weave in ends.
Block as desired.

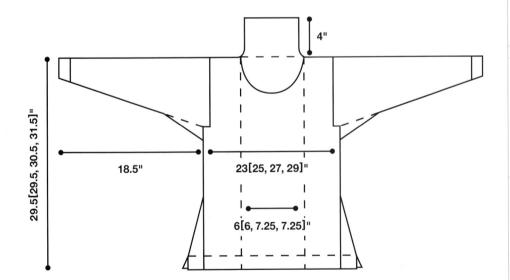

SIZE
L[1X, 2X, 3X]

FINISHED MEASUREMENTS
[in inches]
Chest: 45[52, 57, 63]
Length: 22[22, 24, 24]

MATERIALS
Cascade Pastaza [50% llama,
50% wool ; 132 yds/121 m per
100g skein]

[MC] 010 Rust; 5[5, 6, 7] skeins

[CC1] 050 Orange; 4[5, 5, 6]
skeins

[CC2] 077 Mustard; 1 skein

1 set US #8/5mm needles

1 set US #7/4.5mm needles

1 16-inch US #8/5mm
circular needle

1 16-inch US #7/4.5mm
circular needle

1 16-inch US #6/4mm
circular needle

4 stitch holders

Tapestry needle

GAUGE
18 sts/26 rows = 4 inches in St
stitch over Mosaic pattern on
US #8/5mm needles

18 sts/34 rows = 4 inches in
garter stitch over Mosaic pattern
on US #7/4.5mm needles

Mosaic Sweater

by Kristi Porter

IN THIS CASE, "mosaic" doesn't mean little broken bits of pottery arranged attractively. This mosaic refers to mosaic stitch—a cool way of getting patterning into your knitting without leaving long floats of yarn on the back of your work. If you can knit stripes and slip a stitch, you're all set. The tone-on-tone pattern is great for girls with bellies, since it never lets the eye sit in one spot too long. The slick patterning at wrist and neckline draw your eyes to your extremities. And if you're craving a matching ensemble, check out the skirt that goes with (see page 128).

Pattern

FRONT
*Using US #7/4.5mm needles and MC, CO 101[115, 129, 143] sts.
K 1 row.
Join CC1 and work Rows 1–20 of Mosaic pattern in garter stitch, using MC for Color A and CC1 for Color B.

K 2 rows using CC1.
Using US #8/5mm needles, work in Mosaic pattern in St st, using CC1 for Color A, and MC for Color B.
Cont in patt as set until work measures 13[13, 14, 14] inches (or desired length to armhole), ending with a WS row.

Shape armhole
BO 5[7, 9, 9] sts at beg of next 2 rows.
BO 5[5, 5, 7] sts at beg of next 2 rows.
81 [91, 101, 111] sts rem.
Decrease Row 1 [RS]: K1, k2tog, work in patt as set to last 3 sts, ssk, k1.
Decrease Row 2 [WS]: P1, p2tog tbl, work in patt as set to last 3 sts, p2tog, p1.
Repeat these 2 rows 0[1, 2, 2] times more, then work *Decrease Row 1* 1[0, 0, 1] time more. 75[83, 89, 97] sts rem. *

Cont in patt as set until work measures 6[6, 7, 7] inches from beg of armhole, ending with a WS row.

Shape neckline
Next Row [RS]: K25[28, 31, 34] sts in patt, BO 25[27, 27, 29] sts, work to end in patt.
Next Row [WS]: P25[28, 31, 34] sts in patt. Place rem sts on st holder.

RIGHT FRONT
Next Row [RS]: K1, k2tog, k to end in patt.

Pattern Notes

Be sure that you are knitting to gauge — for some knitters, there is a tendency to pull the floating yarn too tightly when slipping stitches. If you find this is happening, try moving up a needle size.

HOW TO KNIT A MOSAIC PATTERN
When working a mosaic pattern, you will alternate colors every 2 rows (a RS and a WS row in MC, then a RS and a WS row in CC, and so on). You will only be using one strand of yarn at a time. On RS rows, the stitches on the chart in the working color for that row are knit, those in the opposite color are slipped PURLWISE. On the subsequent WS rows, the stitches that were knit in the preceding row are worked in pattern and the slipped stitches are slipped again PURLWISE. Slipped stitches are ALWAYS slipped twice.

Always hold the yarn to the wrong side of work when slipping stitches. When knitting the garter stitch borders, this means that on WS rows, you will have to bring the yarn to the front to slip the stitches and return it to the back for the worked stitches. For the body of the sweater, worked in St st, the yarn will always be on the correct side for slipping the stitches. >>

It is important to maintain the pattern as set when you begin increasing or decreasing. Always work the first and last stitch on any row in the working color for that row; the remainder of the stitches are worked appropriately to maintain the pattern as set. While this might seem complicated at the outset, the pattern is very repetitive (a 13-stitch repeat over 20 rows) and by the time the decreases begin, you will easily be able to see where you are in the pattern.

GREEK CROSS MEDALLION MOSAIC PATTERN
Adapted from Barbara G. Walker's *A Second Treasury of Knitting Patterns*
Worked over a multiple of 14 stitches plus 3.

Cast on using Color A and knit 1 row.
Row 1 [RS]: Using Color B, k2, [sl 1, k1, (sl 1, k3) twice, (sl 1, k1) twice] to last st, k1.
Even-numbered Rows 2–20: Using the same color as the previous row, knit (if working in garter stitch) or purl (if working in St stitch) the stitches worked on previous row, slip all stitches slipped on previous row. *When slipping stitches on a WS row, make sure the yarn is held to the front (the side facing you) of the work!*
Row 3 [RS]: Using Color A, k5, sl1, k5, [sl1, k7, sl1, k5] to last 6 sts, sl1, k5.
Row 5 [RS]: Using Color B, k2, [(sl 1, k3) 3 times, sl 1, k1] to last st, k1.
Row 7 [RS]: Using Color A, k3, [sl 1, k3, sl 1, k1, (sl 1, k3) twice] to end.
Row 9 [RS]: Using Color B, k4, sl1, k7, [sl1, k5, sl1, k7] to last 5 sts, sl1, k4.
Row 11 [RS]: Using Color A, k1, [sl 1, k3, (sl 1, k1) 3 times, sl 1, k3] to last 2 sts, sl1, k1.
Row 13 [RS]: Work as for Row 9.
Row 15 [RS]: Work as for Row 7.
Row 17 [RS]: Work as for Row 5.
Row 19 [RS]: Work as for Row 3.

Repeat *Rows 1–20* for Mosaic Pattern.

Use the row-by-row instructions above over 31 stitches to make your swatch. The chart below contains the same information and will be useful once you become acquainted with the mosaic technique. When you begin making increases or decreases, the chart will help you visualize what comes next.

When reading the chart, the bar at right shows which color is used for each row. In each chart row, the squares in that color indicate stitches to knit, and the squares in the other color indicate stitches to slip. Only RS rows are shown.

Next Row [WS]: P in patt.
Repeat these 2 rows 4[7, 5, 8] times more. 20[20, 25, 25] sts rem.
AT THE SAME TIME, when work measures 8[8, 9, 9] inches from beg of armhole, ending with a WS row, shape shoulders using short rows as follows:
Row 1 [RS]: K in patt to last 5[5, 7, 7] sts, W&T.
Row 2 [WS]: P in patt.
Row 3 [RS]: K in patt to last 10[10, 14, 14] sts, W&T.
Row 4 [WS]: P in patt.
Row 5 [RS]: K in patt to last 15[15, 20, 20] sts, W&T.
Row 6 [WS]: P in patt.
Row 7 [RS]: K in patt. When you encounter a wrapped st, pick up the wrap, place it on the left needle, and k it tog with the wrapped st.
Row 8 [WS]: P in patt. Place all sts on st holder.

LEFT FRONT
Replace held sts for left side of neckline on needle with WS facing and reattach yarn. P in patt.

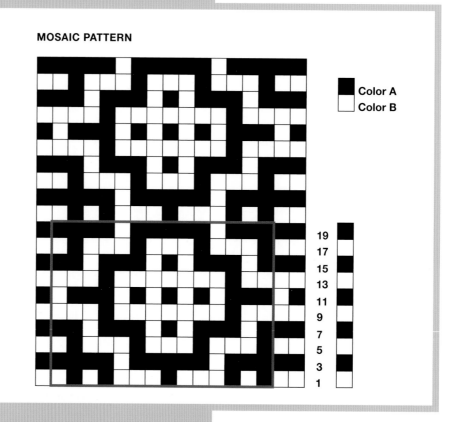

MOSAIC PATTERN

Color A
Color B

19
17
15
13
11
9
7
5
3
1

Next Row [RS]: K to last 3 sts in patt, ssk, k1.
Next Row [WS]: P in patt.
Repeat these 2 rows 4[7, 5, 8] times more. 20[20, 25, 25] sts rem.
AT THE SAME TIME, when work measures 8[8, 9, 9] inches from beg of armhole, ending on a WS row, shape shoulders using short rows as follows:
When working RS rows during the following short-rowed section, you will be instructed to work a certain number of stitches "in stranded pattern." This means that the stitches that would normally be slipped according to the stitch pattern should instead be worked with the yarn not in use for that row. For example, if you are working an MC row, the stitches that would normally be slipped should instead be worked with CC, and vice versa, as if you were working a stranded color pattern. This is done so that the yarn not in use will be in the correct position for the next short row.

Row 1 [RS]: K in patt, working the first 5[5, 7, 7] sts of the row in stranded pattern.
Row 2 [WS]: P in patt to last 5[5, 7, 7] sts, W&T.
Row 3 [RS]: K to end in patt, working the first 5[5, 7, 7] sts of the row in stranded pattern.
Row 4 [WS]: P in patt to last 10[10, 14, 14] sts, W&T.
Row 5 [RS]: K to end in patt working the first 5[5, 6, 6] sts of the row in stranded pattern.
Row 6 [WS]: P in patt to last 15[15, 20, 20] sts, W&T.
Row 7 [RS]: K in patt.
Row 8 [WS]: P in patt. When you encounter a wrapped st, pick up the wrap, place it on the left needle, and p it tog with the wrapped st.
Place all sts on st holder.

BACK
Work as for Front from * to *.

Cont in patt as set until work measures 7[7, 8, 8] inches from beg of armhole, ending with a WS row.

Row 1 [RS]: K25[25, 28, 30] sts in patt, BO 25[33, 33, 37] sts, work to end in patt.
Row 2 [WS]: P25[25, 28, 30] sts in patt. Place rem sts on st holder.

Row 3 [RS]: K1, k2tog, k to end in patt.
Row 4 [WS]: P in patt.
Repeat these 2 rows 4[4, 2, 4] times more. 20[20, 25, 25] sts rem.
AT THE SAME TIME, when work measures 8[8, 9, 9] inches from beg of armhole, ending on a WS row, shape shoulders using short rows as for Right Front.
Place all sts on st holder.

Replace held sts from left side of neckline on needle with WS facing and reattach yarn. P in patt.
Next Row [RS]: K to last 3 sts in patt, ssk, k1.
Next Row [WS]: P in patt.
Repeat these 2 rows 4[4, 2, 4] times more. 20[20, 25, 25] sts rem.
AT THE SAME TIME, when work measures 8[8, 9, 9] inches from beg of armhole, ending on a WS row, shape shoulders using short rows as for Left Front.
Place all sts on st holder.

SLEEVES (MAKE 2)
Using US #7/4.5mm needles and CC2, CO 45[45, 59, 59] sts.
K 1 row.
Join MC and work Rows 1–20 of Mosaic Pattern in garter stitch, using CC2 for Color A and MC for Color B.

K 2 rows using CC2. Break CC2 and join CC1.
Using US #8/5mm needles, work in Mosaic pattern in St st, using CC1 for Color A, and MC for Color B.
Work 3 rows in patt as set, ending with a WS row.

Next row [RS]: K1, m1, k in patt to last st, m1, k1.
Work 3 rows in patt as set, incorporating new sts into patt.
Repeat these 4 rows 12[12, 10, 10] times more. 71[71, 81, 81] sts.

Cont in patt as set until work measures 14 inches (or desired length), ending with a WS row.

BO 5[7, 9, 9] sts at beg of next 2 rows.
BO 5[5, 5, 7] sts at beg of next 2 rows.
51[47, 53, 49] sts rem.

Next Row [RS]: K1, k2tog, work in patt as set to last 3 sts, ssk, k1.
Next Row [WS]: P all sts in patt as set.
Repeat these 2 rows 14[13, 15, 14] times more. 21[19, 21, 19] sts rem.

BO all sts.

Finishing

A piece worked in a mosaic pattern benefits from a thorough blocking. If you have made this in Pastaza or another appropriate yarn (if in doubt, test on your swatch!) you can press this with a damp cloth and an iron set to "wool" with no ill effects. This will smooth out any bumpiness and make seaming easier. If you're squeamish about the iron, give the pieces a good damp blocking before seaming.

Use Three-Needle Bind Off to attach shoulder seams.
Sew sleeve caps into armholes.
Sew sleeve seams and side seams, leaving bottom 2.5 inches of side seam open.
Starting at one shoulder seam and with RS facing, using US #8/5mm circular needle and CC1, pick up and k 1 st in each st and 1 st in every 2 rows around neckline. P 1 round. Break yarn.
Using US #7/4.5mm circular needle and CC2, k 1 round, then p 1 round. Break yarn.
Using US #6/4mm circular needle and MC, k1 round, then p 1 round.
BO all sts loosely.
Weave in ends.

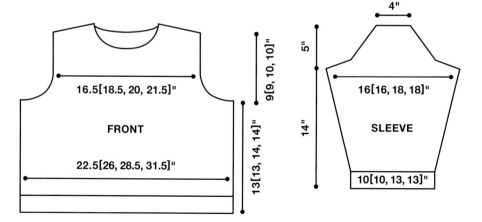

chapter 6

Sandy Cardigan

Lift and Separate

Chocolate-Covered Cherry Jacket

Natalie Coat

Cardigans and Coats

Curvalicious Cardigan

Meryl Coat

SIZE

Custom-fit to individual measurements.
L[1X, 2X, 3X]

FINISHED MEASUREMENTS

Chest: actual bust plus 4 inches of ease
Length: 27 inches

MATERIALS

[MC] Brown Sheep Lamb's Pride Worsted [85% wool, 15% mohair; 190 yds/171 m per 100g skein]; color: M185 Aubergine; 4[5, 5, 6] skeins.

[CC] Noro Kureyon [100% wool; 109 yds/100 m per 50g skein]; color: 148; 8 skeins
Seven skeins of Kureyon will provide sufficient yardage, but the extra skein will enable you to keep the continuity of the color sequence.

1 set US #8/5mm double-pointed needles

1 24-inch US #8/5mm circular needle

1 40-inch US #8/5mm circular needle

Waste yarn

Stitch markers

Safety pins

Tapestry needle

9 ¾-inch buttons
(See Shop Till You Drop, page 157)

GAUGE

16 sts/32 rows = 4 inches in garter stitch

Sandy Cardigan

by Emma Crew

SELF-STRIPING YARN IS ENTICING, but it can give the wrong message: a horizontal one. This smart cardigan avoids that and gives you maximum impact without maximum yardage. The diagonal stripes don't let the eye stay in one place for long…a nice camouflage for tum and tush. Solid side panels are cleverly contoured to create the impression of a waist, whether you have one or not. And with just a little well-placed math, you can shape the panels to your own measurements for a custom fit.

Pattern

BACK DIAGONAL PANELS (MAKE 2)
*Using shorter circular needle or straight needles and CC, CO 2 sts.

Increase section
Row 1: K1, kfb.
Increase Row: K1, kfb, k to end.
Repeat *Increase Row* 36 times more.
40 sts.

Straight section
Row 1: K1, kfb, k to last 3 sts, k2tog, k1.
Row 2: K all sts.
Repeat these 2 rows 56 times more. 75 garter ridges along long edge of panel.*

Decrease section
Decrease Row: K to last 3 sts, k2tog, k1.
Repeat this row 36 times more. 3 sts rem.

Next Row: K2tog, k1.
Next Row: K2tog. Break yarn and draw through rem st.

FRONT DIAGONAL PANELS (MAKE 2)
Work as for Back Diagonal Panels from * to *. If more length is desired for the front of the sweater to accommodate a full bust, work 6 additional rows (3 additional garter ridges) for each additional inch desired, or 1[2, 3, 4] inches longer (6[12, 18, 24] more rows) for B[C, D, DD] cup.

Decrease section
Decrease Row: K to last 3 sts, k2tog, k1.
Repeat this row 5 times more. 34 sts rem.

Place sts on holder or waste yarn. Sew Back Panels together along one long edge, with garter ridges arranged to form a chevron.
Diagonal panels are reversible. If designated a RS and WS while working the panels, you will now use one panel with the RS showing, and one with the WS showing. A RS will need to be designated for the joined back panel before proceeding to the next step.

This garment is designed so that each Diagonal Panel with added Vertical Side Panel is 9 inches wide. Without the Shaped Side Panels, the garment would be 36 inches around, with 18 inches from shoulder to shoulder.

If you have particularly wide or narrow shoulders, these panels can be knit to a different width by working the increases on each diagonal panel until one short edge of the triangle is the desired width of the diagonal panel. Subtract your desired amount of ease from the total width of all 4 panels, and use this number instead of 32 in the formulas for A, B, and C. When changing the length of the garment, formulas F and G must be changed as follows: Multiply the desired length in inches from lower edge of garment to natural waist by 8. Use this number in place of 72 for formulas F and G.

VERTICAL SIDE PANELS

With RS facing, using MC and longer circular needle, pick up and k 7 sts for every 5 garter ridges along one long edge of Back Panel. 105 sts. K 15 rows, place sts on st holder.

Repeat for other long edge of Back Panel.

With RS facing, beg at top of long edge of Right Front Panel, pick up and k 7 sts for every 5 garter ridges along one long edge of Right Front Panel; 105 sts plus approx. 4 sts for each additional inch of length of Front Panel.

If no extra length has been added to Front Panels, k 15 rows, place sts on st holder or waste yarn.

If extra length has been added, proceed as follows:

In a mirror, position top of panel at shoulder, where shoulder seam would fall, so that front of panel is at center front of your torso. Place a safety pin in the outer edge of the panel at the level of your bust point.

Next Row [WS]: K to pin, place marker, k to end. Remove pin. Make a note of number of sts between marker, and top of panel.

If 1 inch has been added (109 sts):
Next Row [RS]: K to marker, k2tog, k to end.
K 3 rows.
Repeat these 4 rows twice more, then work the first 2 of these rows once more. 105 sts rem. Place sts on st holder or waste yarn.

If 2 inches have been added (113 sts):
Next Row [RS]: K to marker, k2tog, k to end.
K 1 row.
Repeat these 2 rows 5 times more.

Next Row [RS]: K to marker, k3tog, k to end.
K 1 row. 105 sts rem. Place sts on st holder or waste yarn.

If 3 inches have been added (117 sts):
Next Row [RS]: K to marker, k2tog, k to end.
Next Row [WS]: K to 2 sts before marker, k2tog, k to end.
Repeat these 2 rows 5 times more. 105 sts rem.

K 2 rows. Place sts on st holder or waste yarn.

If 4 inches have been added (121 sts):
Next Row [RS]: K to marker, k2tog, k to end.
Next Row [WS]: K to 2 sts before marker, k2tog, k to end.
Repeat these 2 rows once more.

Next Row [RS]: K to marker, k3tog, k to end.
Next Row [WS]: K to 2 sts before marker, k2tog, k to end.
Repeat from * once more.

Next Row [RS]: K to marker, k2tog, k to end.
Next Row [WS]: K to 2 sts before marker, k2tog, k to end.
105 sts rem. Place sts on st holder or waste yarn.

All sizes:
Repeat for Left Front Panel, but pick up sts beg at bottom of panel. If length has been added, work decreases as above, but work them on the opposite side of the marker. (ie. Work in last 2 sts before marker on RS rows, after marker on WS rows.)
Sew shoulder seams, matching tops of panels.

SHAPED SIDE PANELS
Calculate side panel shaping

These formulas use your actual hip, bust and waist measurements in inches, and include 4 inches of ease. Take your measurements before proceeding, then use them to calculate values for the following variables:

A = (Hip ÷ 32) x 2 = number of sts to CO at lower edge of gusset

B = (Waist ÷ 32) x 2 = number of gusset sts at waist

C = (Bust ÷ 32) x 2 = number of gusset sts at fullest point of bust

D = (**A** ÷ **B**) = number of sts to be decreased from hip to waist
*[If **D** is a negative number, work increases instead of decreases.]*

E = (**D** ÷ 2) = number of decrease rows to be worked

F = (72 ÷ **D**) *(round down to nearest even number)* = number of rows to be worked for this decrease section

G = (72 ÷ (**E** x **F**)) = number of rows to be knit without shaping before waist decreases begin

H = (**C** ÷ **B**) = number of sts to be increased from waist to bust
*[If **H** is a negative number, work decreases instead of increases.]*

J = (**H** ÷ 2) = number of increase rows to be worked

K = (50 ÷ **J**) *(round down to nearest even number)* = number of rows to be worked for this increase section

L = (60 ÷ (**J** x **K**)) = number of rows to be worked without shaping after increase rows *(**L** will be equal to or greater than 10)*

Set up shaped side panels

Shaped Side Panels are joined to Vertical Side Panels as they are worked. On each RS row, the first and last sts of the Shaped Panel will be worked together with sts from the Vertical Panels. Switch to shorter circular needle, then double-pointed needles, as necessary.

Using MC and longer circular needle, CO ____**A** sts.

Set-up Row [RS]: K1, place marker, k to last st, place marker, k last st of Shaped Panel, k all sts of Right Back Vertical Panel, k to last st of Right Front Vertical Panel. Hold beg and end of Set-up Row tog as if to beg working in the round.

Row 1 [RS]: K first st of Shaped Panel tog with last st of Vertical Panel, k to marker, ssk (last st of Shaped Panel

worked tog with first st of Vertical Panel). Turn work.
Row 2 [WS]: Sl1, k to marker, sl1.
Turn work.
Repeat these 2 rows until ____**G** rows have been worked.

Decrease Row [RS]: K2tog, k2tog, k to 2 sts before marker, ssk, ssk. Turn work.
Work *Row 2* as above.
Work *Rows 1* and *2* as above for ____ (**F÷2**) rows.
Repeat these ____**F** rows ____ (**E÷1**) times more.
(____**E** decrease rows have been worked. 72 rows have been worked in total; 36 garter ridges.)

Increase Row [RS]: K2tog, kfb, k to last st before marker, kfb, ssk. Turn work.
Work *Row 2* as above.
Work *Rows 1* and *2* as above for ____ (**K÷2**) rows.
Repeat these ____**K** rows ____ (**J÷1**) times more. (____**J** decrease rows have been worked.)

Work *Rows 1* and *2* as above for ____**L** rows. 132 rows (66 garter ridges) have been worked.
____(**C÷2**) sts between markers, 80 sts on rest of needle.

SLEEVE CAP

Next Row [RS]: K sts between markers, k43. *You should be 3 sts past the shoulder seam.* W&T.
K6, W&T.
K9, W&T.
Work 23 more short rows, working each short row 3 sts longer than the last. The last 2 of these short rows will be:
K75, W&T.
K78, W&T.

K79 (to first Shaped Panel marker), k to center of sts between markers. Turn work, this point will be the beginning of row. *The sleeve will be worked back and forth in garter st, then seamed during the finishing process. You may wish to switch to the shorter circular needle at this point.*

UNDERARM GUSSET
Next Row: K to 2 sts before marker, ssk, k to second marker, k2tog, k to end. Repeat this row until 1 st rem at either end of row, outside markers; remove markers on last row. 82 sts rem.

K 5 or 6 rows, ending with a WS row. *Whether you need 5 or 6 rows to end with a WS row will depend on how many Side Panel sts you had.*

Next Row [RS]: K1, k2tog, k to last 3 sts, ssk, k1.
K 5 rows.
Repeat these 6 rows 20 times more. 40 sts rem.

Cont in garter stitch until sleeve measures 18–20 inches from beg of underarm gusset, or desired length, ending with a WS row. BO by working Applied i-cord over sleeve sts.

Work Left Shaped Side Panel and Sleeve in the same way.

COLLAR
Using MC and shorter circular needle, with RS facing, k 34 held sts from Right Front Diagonal Panel, k1 in end of shoulder seam, place marker, pick up and k 28 sts (7 sts for every 5 garter ridges) along Right Back Diagonal Panel, place marker, pick up and k 28 sts along Left Back Diagonal Panel, place marker, k1 in end of shoulder seam, k 34 held sts from Left Front Diagonal Panel. 126 sts.
K 1 row.

Next Row [RS]: K to 2 sts before first marker, ssk, k2tog, k to 3 sts after second marker, W&T.
K6, W&T.
K9, W&T.
Work 15 more short rows, working each short row 3 sts longer than the last. The last 2 of these short rows will be:
K51, W&T.
K54, W&T.

K to 2 sts before third marker, ssk, k2tog, k4, W&T.
K66 (to 5 sts after first marker), W&T.
K71, W&T.
K76, W&T.
Work 9 more short rows, working each short row 5 sts longer than the last. The last 2 of these short rows will be:
K116, W&T.
K121, W&T.

K to end.
Set aside.

Finishing

Decide on position for buttons and mark button loop placement on right front side. Place one button at fullest point of bust, one right below collar; space others evenly. Mark location of each button loop with a safety pin. Beg at lower edge at base of center back seam, with RS facing, using longer circular needle and MC, pick up sts around entire lower, front, and collar edges of garment; along lower edge of right side, up right front edge, k 1 row across all collar sts, cont down left front edge and along lower left edge to center back. Pick up 7 sts for every 5 garter ridges along Diagonal Panels, 1 st in each garter ridge along Vertical Panels, and 1 st in each CO st of Shaped Panels. There will likely be more sts than will comfortably fit on one circular needle; do not hesitate to use both circular needles and 2 or 3 of your double-pointed needles; just be sure to leave 2 of your double-pointed needles free for working Applied i-cord.

Work Applied i-cord along lower right edge.

Work 2 rows of i-cord to turn corner.

Work Applied i-cord along right front edge to first button loop marker.

Work 8 rows of i-cord (or long enough piece to fit around button); cont Applied i-cord along right front edge from next picked-up st, working rem

button loops in the same way.

Work 1 row of i-cord to turn corner at edge of collar, BO all collar sts by working Applied i-cord.

Turn corners and work Applied i-cord along left front and lower left edges in the same manner, omitting button loops.

Graft end of i-cord to beg of i-cord.

Weave in ends.

Sew buttons to left front opposite button loops.

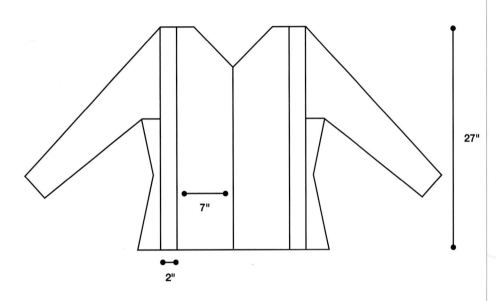

7"

2"

27"

All measurements other than those shown are customized, based on the measurements of the knitter.

SIZE
L[1X, 2X, 3X]

FINISHED MEASUREMENTS
[in inches]
Chest: 41[45, 49, 53]
Hips: 42[46, 50, 54]
Length: 24[24, 25, 26.5]

MATERIALS
Elann Peruvian Collection Pure
Alpaca [100% alpaca, 109
yds/100 m per 50g ball]; color:
Cactus; 15[16, 17, 18] balls

1 set US #5/3.75mm needles

1 set double-pointed needles,
US #5/3.75mm or smaller

Tapestry needle

2.5mm crochet hook

Stitch holders

Waste yarn—a smooth yarn
like mercerized cotton is best

GAUGE
21 sts/26 rows over
4 inches in St stitch

Lift and Separate

by Amy M. Swenson

THE WRAP IS, AS WE'VE SAID MORE THAN ONCE, *THE* sweater for Big Girls. This one is in luscious alpaca that drapes where you want it to, but still holds its shape. The strong diagonal lines of the wrap are adjustable to give you anything from a modest V neck to *va-va-va-voom.* Wear it tied on the side, or just secure the ties flat with a gorgeous pin.

Pattern

BACK

You will work the bottom band, turn work 90 degrees and work the back up from the bottom band.

Using Crochet Cast On, CO 15 sts. Work 141[151, 161, 171] rows in 1 x 1 Rib, ending with a RS row.

Place first 14 sts of row just worked on st holder; 1 st rem on needle.

Pick up and k 4 sts in every 5 rows along edge of work; 113[121, 129, 137] sts, incl. st left on needle from last row worked.

P 1 row.

Next Row [RS]: K20, place marker, k73[81, 89, 97], place marker, k20.

Cont in St st until work measures 3.5 inches from picked-up sts (top edge of ribbed band), ending with a WS row.

Next Row [RS]: K to marker, k2tog, k to 2 sts before marker, ssk, k to end.

Work 3 rows in St st.

Repeat these 4 rows 4 times more. 103[111, 119, 127] sts rem.

Cont in St st until work measures 7.5[7.5, 8.5, 9.5] inches from picked-up sts, ending with a WS row.

Next Row [RS]: K to marker, slip marker, m1, k to marker, m1, slip marker, k to end.

Work 3 rows in St st.

Repeat these 4 rows 2 times more, removing markers on last row. 109[117, 125, 133] sts.

Cont in St st until work measures 12.5[12.5, 13.5, 14.5] inches from picked-up sts, ending with a WS row.

Shape armholes

BO 6[7, 7, 8] sts at beg of next 2 rows. 97[103, 111, 117] sts rem.

BO 3[3, 3, 4] sts at beg of next 2 rows. 91[97, 105, 109] sts rem.

Next Row [RS]: K1, k2tog, k to last 3 sts, ssk, k1.

P 1 row.

Repeat these 2 rows 6[7, 8, 9] times more. 77[81, 87, 89] sts rem.

Pattern Notes

This alpaca wrap cardigan is soft and flowy and can be worn loose in front, or more snug as desired. The measurements given for the hips and bust are with the sweater fully closed. For the best fit, choose a size that is close to your actual measurements. When worn properly, the sweater will have an additional 2 to 5 inches of ease on the front. Because the sweater can be adjusted, the sides require minimal shaping.

1 X 1 RIB (Worked over an odd number of sts):
Row 1 [RS]: K1, [p1, k1] to end.
Row 2 [WS]: P1, [k1, p1] to end.
Repeat these 2 rows for
1 x 1 Rib.

CROCHET CAST ON: Using waste yarn, work a crochet chain several sts longer than the number of sts to be cast on. Starting 1 or 2 sts in from end of chain and using working yarn, pick up and k 1 st in the back loop of each st until the required number of sts have been worked. Later, the chain will be unraveled and the resulting live sts picked up.

Cont in St st until armhole measures 10[10, 10, 10.5] inches from first armhole BO row, ending with a WS row.

SHAPE NECK AND SHOULDERS
Left neck and shoulder
Row 1 [RS]: K25[27, 30, 31], BO 27 sts, k to end.
Row 2 [WS]: P25[27, 30, 31], place rem sts on st holder.
Row 3 [RS]: BO 3 sts, k to end. 22[24, 27, 28] sts rem.
Row 4: P.
Row 5 [RS]: K1, k2tog, k13[14, 16, 17], W&T. P to end.
Row 6 [RS]: K1, k2tog, k6[6, 7, 7], W&T. P to end.
Row 7 [RS]: K1, k2tog, k to end; when you encounter a wrapped st, pick up the wrap and place it on the left needle, then k it tog with the wrapped st. 19[21, 24, 25] sts rem.
Row 8: P.
BO all sts.

Right neck and shoulder
Replace held sts from right shoulder on needle with RS facing, and rejoin yarn.
Row 1: K.
Row 2 [WS]: BO 3 sts, p to end. 22[24, 27, 28] sts rem.
Row 3: K.
Row 4 [WS]: P1, p2tog tbl, p13[14, 16, 17], W&T. K to end.
Row 5 [RS]: P1, p2tog tbl, P6[6, 7, 7], W&T. K to end.
Row 6 [RS]: P1, p2tog tbl, p to end; when you encounter a wrapped st, pick up the wrap and place it on the left needle, then p it tog with the wrapped st. 19[21, 24, 25] sts rem.
Row 7: K.
BO all sts.

LEFT FRONT
Read through pattern carefully before beginning! Different sets of shaping are worked simultaneously.
Fronts are worked without ribbing; it will be worked later and sewn to Fronts during Finishing.

CO 77[83, 89, 95] sts.
Row 1 [WS]: P57[63, 69, 75], place marker, p20.
Row 2 [RS]: K to last st, m1, k1.
Row 3: P.
Repeat *Rows 2 and 3* 17 times more.
AT THE SAME TIME: When work measures 3.5 inches, ending with a WS row, decrease for waist shaping as follows:
Next Row [RS]: K to marker, k2tog, k to end.
Work 3 rows in St st.
Repeat these 4 rows 4 times more.
AT THE SAME TIME: When all 36 shaping rows at front edge are complete, shape front edge as follows:
Row 1 [RS]: K to end, CO 5 sts.
Row 2: P.
Row 3: K.
Row 4 [WS]: BO 7 sts, p to end.
Row 5 [RS]: K to last st, sl 1.
Row 6 [WS]: BO 5 sts, p to end.

Front edge
Set aside work momentarily and make a crochet chain at least 11 sts long, using waste yarn.
Row 1 [RS]: K to end; CO 7 sts using Crochet/Provisional Cast On (with the chain you just made) at the end of this row.
Row 2 [WS]: Work Row 2 of 1 x 1 Rib over 7 sts, place marker, p to end.

Row 3 [RS]: K to 3 sts before marker, k2tog, k1, work in 1 x 1 Rib to end.
Row 4 [WS]: Work in 1 x 1 Rib to marker, p to end.
Repeat *Rows 3 and 4* 50[52, 54, 56] times more.
AT THE SAME TIME: When work measures 7.5[7.5, 8.5, 9.5] inches, increase for waist shaping as follows:
Next Row [RS]: K to marker, slip marker, m1, k to end.
Work 3 rows in St st.
Repeat these 4 rows 2 times more.

Cont in patt, working front edge shaping as set, until work measures 12.5[12.5, 13.5, 14.5] inches, ending with a WS row.

Shape armhole

Row 1 [RS]: BO 6[7, 7, 8] sts, work to end in patt.
Row 2 [WS]: Work in patt as set.
Row 3 [RS]: BO 3[3, 3, 4] sts, work to end in patt.
Row 4 [WS]: Work in patt as set.
Row 5 [RS]: K1, k2tog, work to end in patt.
Row 6 [WS]: Work in patt as set.
Repeat *Rows 5 and 6* 6[7, 8, 9] times more.

Cont in patt as set until armhole measures 10[10, 10, 10.5] inches from first armhole BO row, ending with a RS row. Once all front shaping decreases have been worked, 26[28, 31, 32] sts rem.

Shape shoulder

Work short rows as follows, beg with a WS row:
Work 19[21, 23, 23] sts in patt as set, W&T. Work in patt to end.
Work 13[14, 15, 15] sts in patt as set, W&T. Work in patt to end.
Work all sts in patt as set; when you encounter a wrapped st, pick up the wrap and place it on the left needle, then p it tog with the wrapped st.
Next Row [RS]: Work in patt as set.
Next Row [WS]: Work 7 sts in rib as set, BO rem 19[21, 24, 25] sts.
Place rib sts on st holder.

RIGHT FRONT

CO 77[83, 89, 95] sts.
Row 1 [WS]: P20, place marker, p57[63, 69, 75].
Row 2 [RS]: K1, m1, k to last st.
Row 3: P.
Repeat *Rows 2 and 3* 17 times more.
AT THE SAME TIME: When work measures 3.5 inches, ending with a WS row, decrease for waist shaping as follows:
Next Row [RS]: K 2 sts before to marker, ssk, k to end.
Work 3 rows in St st.
Repeat these 4 rows 4 times more.
AT THE SAME TIME: When all 36 shaping rows at front edge are complete, shape front edge as follows:

Row 1 [RS]: K.
Row 2 [WS]: P to end, CO 5 sts.
Row 3 [RS]: K.
Row 4 [WS]: P.
Row 5 [RS]: BO 7 sts, k to end.
Row 6 [WS]: P to last st, sl 1.
Row 7 [RS]: BO 5 sts, k to end.

Front edge

Set aside work momentarily and make a crochet chain at least 11 sts long, using waste yarn.
Row 1 [WS]: P to end; CO 7 sts using Crochet/Provisional Cast On (with the chain you just made) at the end of this row.
Row 2 [RS]: Work 7 sts in 1 x 1 Rib, place marker, k to end.

Row 3 [WS]: P to marker, work in 1 x 1 Rib to end.
Row 4 [RS]: Work in 1 x 1 Rib to marker, k1, ssk, k to end.
Repeat *Rows 3 and 4* 50[52, 54, 56] times more.
AT THE SAME TIME: When work measures 7.5[7.5, 8.5, 9.5] inches, increase for waist shaping as follows:
Next Row [RS]: K to marker, m1, slip marker, k to end.
Work 3 rows in St st.
Repeat these 4 rows 2 times more.

Cont in patt, working front edge shaping as set, until work measures 12.5[12.5, 13.5, 14.5] inches, ending with a RS row.

Shape armhole

Row 1 [WS]: BO 6[7, 7, 8] sts, work to end in patt.
Row 2 [RS]: Work in patt as set.
Row 3 [WS]: BO 3[3, 3, 4] sts, work to end in patt.

Row 4 [RS]: Work in patt to last 3 sts, ssk, k1.
Row 5 [WS]: Work in patt as set.
Repeat *Rows 4 and 5* 6[7, 8, 9] times more.

Cont in patt as set until armhole measures 10[10, 10, 10.5] inches from first armhole BO row, ending with a WS row. Once all front shaping decreases have been worked, 26[28, 31, 32] sts rem.

Shape shoulder
Work short rows as follows, beg with a RS row:
Work 19[21, 23, 23] sts in patt as set, W&T. Work in patt to end.
Work 13[14, 15, 15] sts in patt as set, W&T. Work in patt to end.
Work all sts in patt as set; when you encounter a wrapped st, pick up the wrap and place it on the left needle, then k it tog with the wrapped st.
Next Row [WS]: Work in patt as set.
Next Row [RS]: Work 7 sts in rib as set, BO rem 19[21, 24, 25] sts.
Place rib sts on holder.

SLEEVES (MAKE 2)
CO 15 sts.
Work 68[74, 78, 84] rows in 1 x 1 Rib, ending with a WS row.
BO all sts, but do not break yarn; 1 st rem on needle.
Pick up and k 4 sts in every 5 rows along edge of work; 55[59, 63, 67] sts picked up, 56[60, 64, 68] sts on needle including working st from BO.
Work 4 inches in St st, ending with a WS row.

Increase Row [RS]: K3, m1, k to last 3 sts, m1, k3.
Work 5 rows in St st.
Repeat these 6 rows 5 times more. 68[72, 76, 80] sts.

Work *Increase Row* as above.
Work 3 rows in St st.
Repeat these 4 rows 9 times more. 88[92, 96, 100] sts.

Cont in St st until sleeve measures 18[18, 19, 20] inches, or desired length to underarm.

Shape sleeve cap
BO 6[7, 7, 8] sts at beg of next 2 rows. 76[78, 82, 84] sts rem.
BO 3[3, 3, 4] sts at beg of next 2 rows. 70[72, 76, 76] sts rem.

Decrease Row [RS]: K1, k2tog, k to last 3 sts, ssk, k1.
P 1 row.
Repeat these 2 rows 9[11, 15, 14] times more. 50[48, 44, 46] sts rem.

Work *Decrease Row* as above.
Work 3 rows in St st.
Repeat these 4 rows 3[2, 0, 2] times more. 42[42, 42, 40] sts rem.

BO 2 sts at beg of next 4 rows. 34[34, 34, 32] sts rem.

BO 5[5, 5, 4] sts at beg of next 4 rows. 14[14, 14, 16] sts rem.

BO rem sts.

Finishing

Lightly steam or wet block pieces.
Sew shoulder seams.
Sew right side seam.
For left side seam, only sew top 5 inches together, and bottom 5 inches together, leaving a gap in the middle. This will become the tie hole after the ties are knitted on. Leaving extra room now will allow you to adjust the position of the hole, to be sure it is in the most comfortable and flattering place for you.

RIBBED EDGES AND TIE
Remove crochet chain from CO edge at bottom left corner of back. Place sts on needle and work in 1 x 1 Rib until ribbed piece is long enough to reach along curved bottom edge of left front, ending with a WS row. Place sts on hold on a double-pointed needle.

Remove crochet chain from CO edge of ribbed sts on left front neckline edge. Place sts on needle and work in 1 x 1 Rib until work reaches point of left front edge, ending with a WS row. Place sts on hold on a double-point needle.

Sew ribbed pieces to edges of left front. Do this before proceeding to next step, so length of ribbed pieces can be adjusted if necessary.

Next Row [RS]: Work first 6 sts from upper ribbed piece, work last st from upper ribbed piece tog with first held st from lower ribbed piece, work rem sts from lower ribbed piece. 21 sts.
Cont in patt as set until work measures 14 inches from join, or desired length. BO all sts.

Work Ribbed Edges and Tie for right front in the same way.
Sew sleeve seams. Sew sleeve caps into armholes.
Try on sweater and position wraps as desired. Mark appropriate position for side tie hole, and finish sewing side seam to edges of tie hole.

Work one row of single crochet around edge of hole to prevent curling.

Place held sts at top edge of ribbed band on Right Front in needle. Work in 1 x 1 Rib until band reaches center back of neck, BO all sts.
Work held sts from ribbed band on left front in the same way.
Sew ends of bands together and sew edges to back neck.
Weave in ends.

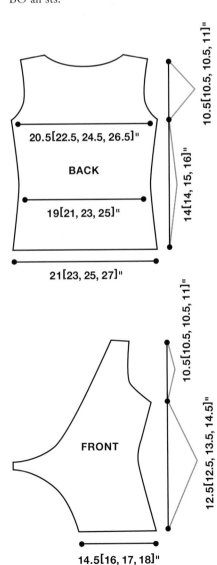

BACK

20.5[22.5, 24.5, 26.5]"

19[21, 23, 25]"

21[23, 25, 27]"

10.5[10.5, 10.5, 11]"

14[14, 15, 16]"

FRONT

10.5[10.5, 10.5, 11]"

12.5[12.5, 13.5, 14.5]"

14.5[16, 17, 18]"

SLEEVE

17[17.5, 18, 18.5]"

18[18, 19, 20]"

11[11.5, 12, 12.5]"

SIZE
L[1X, 2X, 3X]

FINISHED MEASUREMENTS
[in inches]
Bust: 44[48, 52, 56]
Hip: 48[52, 56, 60]
Length: 37

MATERIALS
Tahki Donegal Tweed Homespun
[100% wool; 183 yds/167 m per
100g skein]; color: 892 green;
9[9, 10, 11] skeins

1 set US #9/5.5mm needles

Stitch markers

Tapestry needle

Approx. 8 inches of hook and
eye tape

Sewing needle

Sewing thread

GAUGE
16 sts/24 rows =
4 inches in St stitch
*It is important to achieve correct
Row Gauge as well as Stitch
Gauge for this pattern.*

Natalie Coat

by Libby Baker

A BIG GIRL'S BEST ACCESSORY CAN BE a knitted coat. This uber-sexy model comes with a deep V neck and lean lapels, all to highlight and streamline what boob girls have got. The fit-and-flare shape is perfect for boob AND butt girls. Pattern interest at the edges and hem will help visually balance the rest of you. And the yarn is so scrumptious, you'll love wrapping yourself in it. If you're a belly girl, check out Meryl…she's for you (see page 77).

Pattern

Read through pattern carefully before beginning! Different sets of shaping are worked simultaneously.

LEFT FRONT
CO 68[72, 76, 80] sts.
Row 1 [RS]: K43[47, 51, 55], place marker, k to end.
Row 2 [WS]: Work Row 2 of Daisy stitch to marker, p to end.
Cont in patt as set for 17 more rows, ending with Row 3 of Daisy stitch.

Next Row [WS]: Work Row 4 of Daisy stitch to 6 sts before marker, p3tog, k3tog, p to end.
Work 17 rows in patt as set.
Repeat these 18 rows 4 times more, then cont in patt as set until work measures 21.75 inches.
AT THE SAME TIME, when work measures 13.5[13.5, 14, 14] inches, ending with a WS row, work waist shaping as follows:

Next Row [RS]: K1, k2tog, work to end of row in patt as set.
Work 3 rows in patt as set.
Repeat these 4 rows 9[9, 7, 7] times more.

Next Row [RS]: K1, m1, work to end of row in patt as set.
Work 3 rows in patt as set.
Repeat these 4 rows 7[7, 5, 5] times more, then cont in patt as set until work measures 26.5[26, 24, 23] inches.
AT THE SAME TIME, when work measures 21.75 inches, ending with a WS row, work neck shaping as follows:
Next Row [WS]: Work in patt as set to marker, remove marker, p to end. *This is the last row of Daisy stitch; cont in St st.*
Next Row [RS]: K to last 4 sts, ssk, k2.
Work 9 rows in St st.
Repeat these 10 rows 8 times more, then cont in St st until armhole shaping is complete and work measures 37 inches.
AT THE SAME TIME, if Short-Row Bust Shaping is desired, use the

instructions in the Pattern Notes section to determine the correct placement for short rows. *This bust shaping is only recommended if you wear a C cup or larger.*

When the appropriate length is reached, ending with a WS row, work Short-Row Bust Shaping as follows:
Row 1 [RS]: K to last 2 sts, W&T.
Row 2: P to last 8 sts, W&T.
Row 3: K to last 4 sts, W&T.
Row 4: P to last 10 sts, W&T.
Row 5: K to last 6 sts, W&T.
Row 6: P to last 12 sts, W&T.
Row 7: K to last 8 sts, W&T.
Row 8: P to last 14 sts, W&T.
Row 9: K to last 10 sts, W&T.
Row 10: P to last 16 sts, W&T.
Row 11: K to last 12 sts, W&T.
Row 12: P to last 18 sts, W&T.
Row 13: K to end of row.
When you encounter a wrapped st, pick up the wrap and place it on the left needle, then k it tog with the wrapped st. Be sure to maintain any neckline or armhole shaping worked on this row.
When purling the next row, be sure to pick up the wrap from the remaining wrapped st and p it tog with the wrapped st.
AT THE SAME TIME, when work measures 26.5[26, 24.5, 23] inches, ending with a WS row, shape armhole as follows:
Row 1 [RS]: BO 2 sts, k to end.
Row 2 [WS]: P all sts.
Row 3 [RS]: K1, k2tog, k to end.
Row 4 [WS]: P all sts.
Repeat *Rows 3 and 4* 30[33, 37, 40] times more. After all shaping is complete, 4[5, 5, 6] sts rem and work measures 37 inches. BO rem sts.

RIGHT FRONT
CO 68[72, 76, 80] sts.
Row 1 [RS]: K25, place marker, k to end.

Row 2 [WS]: P to marker, work Row 2 of Daisy stitch to end.
Cont in patt as set for 17 more rows, ending with Row 3 of Daisy stitch.
Next Row [WS]: P to marker, k3tog, p3tog, cont in Daisy stitch as set to end.
Work 17 rows in patt as set.
Repeat these 18 rows 4 times more, then cont in patt as set until work measures 21.75 inches.
AT THE SAME TIME, when work measures 13.5[13.5, 14, 14] inches, ending with a WS row, work waist shaping as follows:
Next Row [RS]: Work in patt as set to last 3 sts, ssk, k1.
Work 3 rows in patt as set.
Repeat these 4 rows 9[9, 7, 7] times more.

Next Row [RS]: Work in patt as set to last st, m1, k1.
Work 3 rows in patt as set.
Repeat these 4 rows 7[7, 5, 5] times more, then cont in patt as set until work measures 26.5[26, 24, 23] inches.
AT THE SAME TIME, when work measures 21.75 inches, ending with a WS row, work neck shaping as follows:
Next Row [WS]: P to marker, remove marker, work in patt as set to end.
This is the last row of Daisy stitch; cont in St st.
Next Row [RS]: K2, k2tog, k to end.
Work 9 rows in St st.
Repeat these 10 rows 8 times more, then cont in St st until armhole shaping is complete and work measures 37 inches.
AT THE SAME TIME, if Short-Row Bust Shaping is desired, use the instructions in the Pattern Notes section to determine the correct placement for short rows. *This bust shaping is only recommended if you wear a C cup or larger.*

When the appropriate length is reached, ending with a RS row, work Short-Row Bust Shaping as follows:
Row 1 [WS]: P to last 2 sts, W&T.
Row 2: K to last 8 sts, W&T.
Row 3: P to last 4 sts, W&T.
Row 4: K to last 10 sts, W&T.

Row 5: P to last 6 sts, W&T.
Row 6: K to last 12 sts, W&T.
Row 7: P to last 8 sts, W&T.
Row 8: K to last 14 sts, W&T.
Row 9: P to last 10 sts, W&T.
Row 10: K to last 16 sts, W&T.
Row 11: P to last 12 sts, W&T.
Row 12: K to last 18 sts, W&T.
Row 13: P to end of row. When you encounter a wrapped st, pick up the wrap and place it on the left needle, then p it tog with the wrapped st. When knitting the next row, be sure to pick up the wrap from the remaining wrapped st and k it tog with the wrapped st.
AT THE SAME TIME, when work measures 26.5[26, 24.5, 23] inches, ending with a RS row, shape armhole as follows:
Next Row [WS]: BO 2 sts, p to end.
Next Row [RS]: K to last 3 sts, ssk, k1.
Next Row [WS]: P all sts.
Repeat these 2 rows 30[33, 37, 40] times more. After all shaping is complete, 4[5, 5, 6] sts rem and work measures 37 inches. BO rem sts.

BACK

CO 96[104, 112, 120] sts.
Beg with a K row, work in St st until work measures 13.5[13.5, 14, 14] inches, ending with a WS row.

Shape waist

Next Row [RS]: K1, k2tog, k to last 3 sts, ssk, k1.
Work 3 rows in patt as set.
Repeat these 4 rows 9[9, 7, 7] times more. 76[84, 96, 104] sts rem.

Next Row [RS]: K1, m1, k to last st, m1, k1.
Work 3 rows in patt as set.
Repeat these 4 rows 7[7, 5, 5] times more. 92[100, 108, 116] sts rem.

Cont in St st until work measures 26.5[26, 24, 23] inches, ending with a WS row.

Armhole shaping

Row 1 [RS]: BO 2 sts, k to end.
Row 2 [WS]: BO 2 sts, p to end.

Row 3 [RS]: K1, k2tog, k to last 3 sts, ssk, k1.
Row 4 [WS]: P all sts.
Repeat *Rows 3 and 4* 30[33, 37, 40] times more. 26[28, 28, 30] sts rem.
BO rem sts.

SLEEVES (MAKE 2)

CO 36[40, 46, 50] sts.
Beg with a K row, work in St st until work measures 7.25 inches, ending with a WS row.
Next Row [RS]: K1, m1, k to last st, m1, k1.
Work 7 rows in St st.
Repeat these 8 rows 7 times more. 52[56, 62, 66] sts.

Cont in St st until work measures 18.25 inches, ending with a WS row.

Row 1 [RS]: BO 2 sts, k to end.
Row 2 [WS]: BO 2 sts, p to end.

Row 3 [RS]: K1, k2tog, k to last 3 sts, ssk, k1.
Rows 4–6: Work in St st.
Row 7 [RS]: K1, k2tog, k to last 3 sts, ssk, k1.
Row 8 [WS]: P all sts.
Repeat *Rows 3–8* 9[10, 11, 12] times more. 8[8, 10, 10] sts rem.

Sizes L and 1X only:

Work 2 more rows in St st. BO all sts.

Sizes 2X and 3X only:

Next Row [RS]: K1, k2tog, k to last 3 sts, ssk, k1. 8 sts rem.
Work 3 rows in St st. BO all sts.

Finishing

Weave in ends.
Block pieces to measurements given in schematics.
Sew fronts and back to sleeves at armhole edges.
Sew underarm and side seams.

COLLAR

With RS facing, pick up and p 26[28, 28, 30] sts along back neck. *This now becomes the WS of the collar.*

Sizes L and 3X only:

Next Row [RS of collar]: K12[14], k2tog, k to end.

Sizes XL and 2X only:

Next Row [RS of collar]: K14, m1, k to end.

All sizes:

Row 1 [WS]: Work Row 1 of Daisy stitch to end, pick up and p 8 sts along top edge of Right Sleeve.
Row 2 [RS]: K to end, pick up and k 8 sts along top edge of Left Sleeve.

Row 3 [WS]: Work next row of Daisy stitch, pick up and p 8 sts along neckline edge (pick up approx. 3 sts in every 4 rows).
Row 4 [RS]: Work next row of Daisy stitch, pick up and k 8 sts along neckline edge (pick up approx. 3 sts in every 4 rows).
Repeat *Rows 3 and 4* until all sts to beg of neckline shaping have been worked.

Next Row [WS]: Work next row of Daisy stitch.
Next Row [RS]: Pick up but do not work 2 sts at beg of next row, slip these sts to right needle, draw first st over second st to bind it off, continue to BO rem sts pwise, when last st is reached pick up but do not work 2 more sts at end of row, slip first st to right needle and draw last st over it, slip rem st to right needle and draw previous st over it. Break yarn and draw through rem st. Weave in rem ends.
Sew hook and eye tape to inside edge of coat below neckline, along top section of center shaping where only a single daisy is formed in stitch pattern.

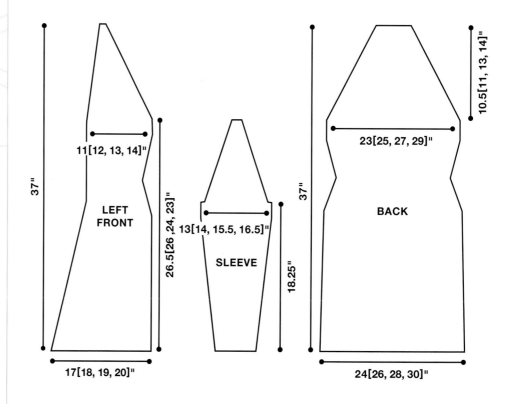

37"

11[12, 13, 14]"

LEFT FRONT

26.5[26 ,24, 23]"

17[18, 19, 20]"

13[14, 15.5, 16.5]"

SLEEVE

18.25"

37"

10.5[11, 13, 14]"

23[25, 27, 29]"

BACK

24[26, 28, 30]"

Meryl Coat

by Libby Baker

ANOTHER CLASSIC COAT WITH ATTITUDE. Meryl features a higher, wider shawl collar than Natalie (page 72), and this draws attention up and away from the bottom Bs (that's belly and butt, in case you haven't read chapter 2) and frames your face. The flyaway shape skims everything, all the way to the hem. You want vertical? We've got vertical lace panels that balance bellies and butts. And the gently flared sleeves are a visual counterbalance to any excess upper armage.

Pattern

Read through pattern carefully before beginning! Different sets of shaping are worked simultaneously.

LEFT FRONT
CO 74[78, 82, 86] sts.
Set-up Row: [RS]: K 41[45, 49, 53] sts, place marker, p1, k3, p1, place marker, work 28 sts in Lace pattern.
*Rows 1, 3, 5, 7, 9 [WS]: Work in Lace pattern to marker, k1, p3, k1, p to end.
Rows 2, 4, 6, 8 [RS]: K to marker, p1, k3, p1, work in Lace pattern to end.
Row 10 [RS]: K to marker, p1, TC, p1, k3tog tbl, [YO, ssk] to last st, k1.
Repeat these 10 rows 4 times more.

Work *Rows 1–9* as above.
Next Row [RS]: K1, k2tog, k to marker, p1, TC, p1, k3tog tbl, [YO, ssk] to last st, k1.*
Repeat from * to * once more. 48[52, 56, 60] sts rem, work measures 20 inches.

Work *Rows 1–9* as above.
Decrease Row 1 [RS]: K to marker, p1, TC, p2tog (remove marker), YO, ssk, k1.
Row 2 [WS]: K1, YO, ssk, k1, p3, k1, p to end.
Row 3 [RS]: K to marker, p1, k3, p1, yo, ssk, k1.
Work *Rows 4–10* in patt as set.
Row 11 [RS]: K to marker, p1, TC, p3tog tbl, k1.
Row 12 [WS]: K2, p3, k1, p to end.
Row 13 [RS]: K to marker, p1, k3, p1, k1.
Work *Rows 14–20* in patt as set.
Remove marker when working last row.
Row 21 [RS]: K to last 3 sts, ssk, k1.
Work *Rows 22–30* in St st.
Repeat *Rows 21–30* 6 times more, then cont in St st until armhole shaping is completed.
AT THE SAME TIME, when work measures 26.5[26, 24, 23] inches, ending with a WS row, shape armhole as follows:

Pattern Notes

LACE PATTERN (Worked over an even number of sts):
Row 1: K1, [YO, ssk] to last st, k1.
Every row is the same.

TC [TURNED CABLE]: Slip next 3 sts onto cable needle, rotate cable needle 180 degrees counter clockwise, k sts from cable needle through back loops.

RTC [REVERSED TURNED CABLE]: Slip next 3 sts onto cable needle, rotate cable needle 180 degrees clockwise, k sts from cable needle through back loops.

K3TOG TBL (OR P3TOG TBL): K (or P) three sts tog through back loops.

SIZE
L[1X, 2X, 3X]

FINISHED MEASUREMENTS
[in inches]
Bust: 44[48, 52, 56]
Hip: 46[50, 54, 58]
Length: 37

MATERIALS
Rowan Yorkshire Tweed Aran
[100% wool; 175 yds/160 m per
100g skein]; color: 410 Wild
Plum; 11[12, 12, 13] skeins

1 set US #9/5.5 mm needles

Stitch markers

Tapestry needle

3 hooks and eyes or hook and
eye tape

Sewing needle

Sewing thread

4 buttons, any size (optional)

3 yds velvet, decorative or
grosgrain ribbon (optional)

GAUGE
16 sts/24 rows =
4 inches in St stitch
*It is important to achieve correct
Row Gauge as well as Stitch
Gauge for this pattern.*

Row 1 [RS]: BO 2 sts, work in patt as set to end.
Row 2 [WS]: Work in patt as set.

Row 3 [RS]: K1, k2tog, work in patt as set to end.
Row 4 [WS]: Work in patt as set.
Repeat *Rows 3 and 4* 30[33, 37, 40] times more. 5[6,6,7] sts rem and work measures 37 inches. BO rem sts.

RIGHT FRONT

CO 74[78, 82, 86] sts.
Set-up Row [RS]: Work 28 sts in Lace pattern, place marker, p1, k3, p1, place marker, k to end.
*Rows 1, 3, 5, 7, and 9 [WS]: P to marker, k1, p3, k1, work in Lace pattern to end.
Rows 2, 4, 6, and 8 [RS]: Work in Lace pattern to marker, p1, k3, p1, k to end.
Row 10 [RS]: Work in Lace pattern to 3 sts before marker, k3tog, p1, RTC, p1, k to end.
Repeat these 10 rows 4 times more.

Work *Rows 1–9* as above.

Next Row [RS]: Work in Lace pattern to 3 sts before marker, k3tog, p1, RTC, p1, k to last 3 sts, ssk, k1.*
Repeat from * to * once more. 48[52, 56, 60] sts rem, work measures 20 inches.

Work *Rows 1–9* as above.

Decrease Row 1 [RS]: K1, YO, ssk, p2tog (remove marker), RTC, p1, k to end.
Row 2 [WS]: P to marker, k1, p3, k1, YO, ssk, k1.
Row 3 [RS]: K1, YO, ssk, p1, k3, p1, k to end.
Rows 4–10: Work in patt as set.
Row 11 [RS]: K1, p3tog, RTC, p1, k to end.
Row 12 [WS]: P to marker, k1, p3, k2.
Row 13 [RS]: K1, p1, k3, p1, k to end.
Rows 14-20: Work in patt as set.
Remove marker when working last row.
Row 21 [RS]: K1, k2tog, k to end.

Rows 22–30: Work in St st.
Repeat *Rows 21–30* 6 times more, then cont in St st until armhole shaping is completed.
AT THE SAME TIME, when work measures 26.5[26, 24, 23] inches, ending with a RS row, shape armhole as follows:

Row 1 [WS]: BO 2 sts, work in patt as set to end.
Row 2 [RS]: Work in patt as set to last 3 sts, ssk, k1.
Row 3 [WS]: Work in patt as set.
Repeat *Rows 2 and 3* 30[33, 37, 40] times more. 5[6, 6, 7] sts rem and work measures 37 inches.
BO rem sts.

BACK

CO 92[100, 108, 116] sts.
Work in St st until work measures 10 inches, ending with a WS row.

Decrease Row [RS]: K1, k2tog, k to last 3 sts, ssk, k1.
Cont in St st until work measures 20 inches, ending with a WS row.

Work *Decrease Row* as above.
Cont in St st until work measures 26.5[26, 24, 23] inches, ending with a WS row.

Row 1 [RS]: BO 2 sts, k to end.
Row 2 [WS]: BO 2 sts, p to end.

Row 3 [RS]: K1, k2tog, k to last 3 sts, ssk, k1.
Row 4 [WS]: P all sts.
Repeat *Rows 3 and 4* 30[33, 37, 40] times more. 22[24, 24, 26] sts rem.
BO rem sts.

SLEEVES (MAKE 2)

CO 42[46, 52, 56] sts.
Set-up Row [RS]: K10[12, 15, 17], place marker, p1, k3, p1, place marker, work 12 sts in Lace pattern, place marker, p1, k3, p1, place marker, k to end.
Rows 1, 3, 5, 7, and 9 [WS]: P to marker, k1, p3, k1, work in Lace

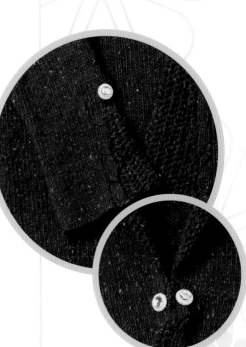

pattern to next marker, k1, p3, k1, p to end.

Rows 2, 4, 6, and 8 [RS]: K to marker, p1, k3, p1, work in Lace pattern to next marker, p1, k3, p1, k to end.

Row 10 [RS]: K to marker, p1, TC, p1, k3tog tbl, [YO, ssk] to 3 sts before next marker, k3tog, p1, RTC, p1, k to end. Repeat these 10 rows.

Repeat *Rows 1–9* once more. Remove second and third markers on *Row 9*.

Next Row [RS]: K to marker, p1, TC, p1, k3tog tbl, k1, p1, RTC, p1, k to end.

Next Row [WS]: P to marker, k1, p3, k2tog twice, p3, k1, p to end. 30[34, 40, 44] sts rem.

Work 8 rows in patt as set. Remove markers on last row.

Next Row [RS]: K1, m1, k to last st, m1, k1.

Work 5 rows in St st.

Repeat these 6 rows 10 times more. 52[56, 62, 66] sts.

Cont in St st until work measures 18.25 inches, ending with a WS row.

Next Row [RS]: BO 2 sts, k to end.
Next Row [WS]: BO 2 sts, p to end.
Next Row [RS]: K1, k2tog, k to last 3 sts, ssk, k1.
Work 3 rows in St st.
Next Row [RS]: K1, k2tog, k to last 3 sts, ssk, k1.
Next Row [WS]: P.
Repeat these 6 rows 9[10, 11, 12] times more. 8[8, 10, 10] sts rem.

Sizes L and 1X only:
Work 2 more rows in St st. BO all sts.

Sizes 2X and 3X only:
Next Row [RS]: K1, k2tog, k to last 3 sts, ssk, k1. 8 sts rem.
Work 3 rows in St st. BO all sts.

COLLAR
CO 4 sts.
K 2 rows.
Set-up Row 1: CO 2, K these 2 sts, k1, YO, ssk, k1.
Set-up Row 2: CO 2, k these 2 sts, k1, [YO, ssk] to last 3 sts, k3.

Rows 1–2: K3, [YO, ssk] to last 3 sts, k3.
Rows 3–4: CO 2, k these 2 sts, k1, [YO, ssk] to last 3 sts, k3.
Repeat *Rows 1–4* 16 times more. 76 sts.

Work *Rows 1–2* as above 20[20, 25, 25] times.

Decrease Row: BO 2, k2, [YO, ssk] to last 3 sts, k3.
Work *Decrease Row* once more.
Work *Rows 1–2* as above.
Repeat these 4 rows 16 times more. 8 sts rem.

Work *Decrease Row* once more.
Next Row: BO 2, YO, ssk, k1. 4 sts rem.
K 2 rows. BO all sts.

Finishing

Weave in ends.
Block pieces to measurements given in schematics.
Sew fronts and back to sleeves at armhole edges.
Sew underarm and side seams.
Sew one long edge of collar to neckline of coat, beginning and ending where lace panels end on fronts of coat.
Fold collar towards inside of coat and sew remaining long edge to inside neckline of coat.
Sew hooks and eyes or hook and eye tape to inside edge of coat below neckline, between last cable twist and end of lace panel.
If using buttons, sew to fronts of jacket below collar, and to sleeves at tops of cable panels, using photo as a guide.
To prevent curling and reinforce hem, sew ribbon along bottom inside edge of coat.

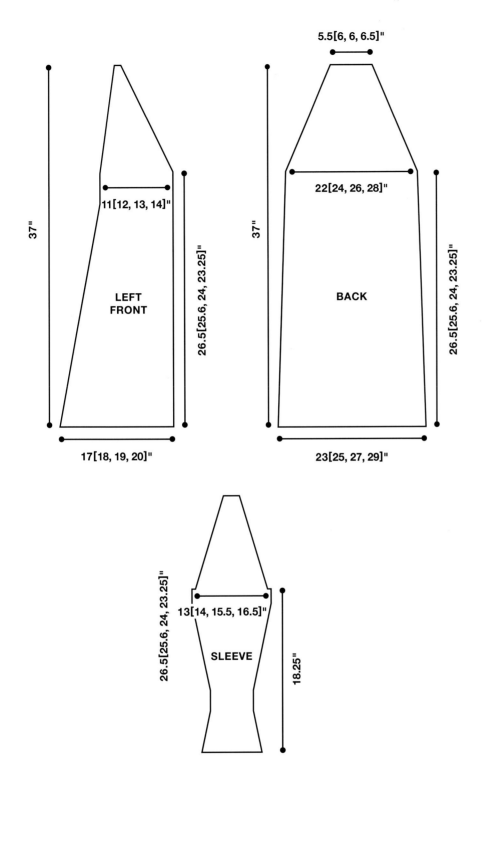

5.5[6, 6, 6.5]"

11[12, 13, 14]"

37"

26.5[25.6, 24, 23.25]"

LEFT
FRONT

17[18, 19, 20]"

22[24, 26, 28]"

37"

26.5[25.6, 24, 23.25]"

BACK

23[25, 27, 29]"

26.5[25.6, 24, 23.25]"

13[14, 15.5, 16.5]"

SLEEVE

18.25"

SIZE
L[1X, 2X, 3X]

FINISHED MEASUREMENTS
[in inches]
Chest: 42[46, 50, 54]
This pattern is meant to be very close fitting. Make the size that is closest to your actual bust measurement.
Length: 21[22.5, 23.5, 24]

MATERIALS
Rowan Calmer, [75% cotton 25% microfiber; 178 yds/160 m per 50g ball]

[MC] 477 Blush; 4[4, 5, 6] skeins

[CC] 481 Coffee Bean; 5[6,7,8] skeins

1 set US #8/5mm double-point needles

1 32-inch US #8/5mm circular needle

1 spare US #8/5mm or smaller circular needle, any length. It will be used to hold stitches.

Stitch markers

Safety pin

Waste yarn or stitch holders

Tapestry needle

Separating zipper, 20[22, 22, 24] inches in length

Sewing thread, same color as MC

Sewing machine or sewing needle

GAUGE
19 sts /24 rows = 4 inches in St stitch

Curvalicious Cardigan

by Jenna Adorno

BLACK may not be the universal answer to "What should I wear?," but that doesn't mean you shouldn't take advantage of dark colors. In this shapely sweater, the dark bits (in espresso brown) are placed deliberately at the sides of the sweater so all you really notice is the bright pop of pink. The fitted shape highlights curves if you've got them, and the shading suggests them if you don't. Boob girls will love the zipper, which delivers as deep a V neck as they can handle.

Pattern

LOWER BODY
I-cord cast on

Using double-pointed needles and MC, CO 3 sts.

Work 50[53, 58, 65] rows of i-cord, join CC, work 25[28, 30, 32] rows using CC, join a new ball of MC, work 100[111, 120, 127] rows using MC, join a new ball of CC, work 25[28, 30, 32] rows using CC, join a new ball of MC, work 50[53, 58, 65] rows using MC. BO all sts, do not break yarn.

When picking up sts in the next row, you will be picking up approx 4 sts for every 5 rows.

Using US #8/5mm circular needle and MC, and beg at end of i-cord using yarn attached, pick up and k 40[43, 47, 52] sts in first section of i-cord, using CC attached pick up and k 20[22, 24, 26] sts in second section of i-cord, using MC attached pick up and k 80[89, 96, 102] sts in third section of i-cord, using

CC attached pick up and k 20[22, 24, 26] sts in fourth section of i-cord, using rem ball of MC attached pick up and k 40[43, 47, 52] sts in last section of i-cord. 200[219, 238, 258] sts.

Knit in St st, working MC sections using MC and CC sections using CC, twisting yarns as described in "Intarsia" section [see Techniques, page 154] until work measures 3[4, 4.5, 5] inches, ending with a WS row.

Waist shaping
Fitting Tip: The waist decreases that follow will bring the waist in six inches. If you desire less waist shaping, work color changes as follows but only work decreases every 6 rows, 5 times in total. This will bring the waist in only 4 inches. Work the corresponding increases as described below, but once again work them every 6 rows, 5 times only.

Row 1 [RS]: [Using MC, k to 1 st before color change in previous row, switch to CC, k to 1 st after color change in previous row, switch to MC] twice, k to end.

Row 2 [WS]: P all sts in colors as set.

Row 3 [RS]: [Using MC, k to 4 sts before color change in previous row, k2tog, k1, switch to CC, k to 1 st after color change in previous row, switch to MC, k1, ssk] twice, k to end.

Row 4 [WS]: P all sts in colors as set.
Repeat these 4 rows 6 times more. 172[191, 210, 230] sts rem.

Waist increase

Row 1 [RS]: [Using MC, k to 1 st after color change in previous row, switch to CC, k to 1 st before color change in previous row, switch to MC,] twice, k to end.

Row 2 [WS]: P all sts in colors as set.

Row 3 [RS]: [Using MC, k to 1 st before color change in previous row, m1, k2, switch to CC, k to 1 st before color change in previous row, switch to MC, k2, m1] twice, k to end.

Row 4 [WS]: P all sts in colors as set.
Repeat these 4 rows 6 times more. 200[219, 238, 258] sts.

Cont in St st with colors as set until work measures 13 [14, 14.5,15] inches, ending with a RS row.

Next Row [WS]: [P to color change using MC, p to next color change using CC, decreasing 0[2, 4, 6] sts evenly spaced in CC section] twice, p to end using MC.

Next Row: K40[43, 47, 52] sts using MC, place next 20 sts on st holder, k80[89, 96, 102] sts using MC, place next 20 sts on st holder, k to end using MC. Set Lower Body aside and work Sleeves.

SLEEVES (MAKE 2)
I-cord cast on

Using double-pointed needles and CC, CO 3 sts.
Work 68[73, 80, 88] rows of i-cord.
BO all sts, do not break yarn.

Pick up and k 54[58, 64, 70] sts along length of i-cord using 3 (or 4 if you have a set of 5) double-pointed needles. Join to begin working in the round and mark beginning of round.
Work in St st until work measures 2[2.5, 2.5, 3]inches.

Next Round: K1, m1, k to last st, m1, k1.
K 4 rounds.
Repeat these 5 rounds 9 times more. 74[78, 84, 90] sts.

Cont in St st until work measures 16[17, 18, 18] inches (or desired length).

K 10 sts and place 20 sts just worked (last 10 sts of previous round and 10 sts of current round) on holder. Slip remaining sts to spare circular needle. Set aside and make second sleeve. After slipping sts to holder after final round of second sleeve, leave rem sts on needles.

Join sleeves to lower body

With RS facing and using MC, k first 40[43, 47, 52] sts of body, using CC k54 [58, 64, 70] of one sleeve onto circular needle (remember to twist yarns to join pieces!), using MC k next 80[89, 96, 102] sts of body, using CC k54[58, 64, 70] of rem sleeve onto circular needle, using MC k rem 40[43, 47, 52] sts of body. 268[291, 318, 346] sts.
P 1 row, working colors as set.

Decrease Row 1 [RS]: [Using MC, k to 3 sts before color change, k2tog, k1, using CC, ssk, k to 2 sts before color change, k2tog, using MC, k1, ssk] twice, k to end.

Decrease Row 2 [WS]: [Using MC, p to 3 sts before color change, p2tog, p1, using CC, p2tog tbl, p to 2 sts before color change, p2tog, using MC, p1, p2tog tbl] twice, p to end.
Repeat these 2 rows 2[2, 4, 7] times more. 220 [243, 238, 281] sts.

Work *Decrease Row 1.*

P 1 row, working colors as set.

Decrease Row 3 [RS]: [Using MC k to color change, using CC ssk, k to 2 sts before color change, k2tog] twice, using MC, k to end.

P 1 row, working colors as set.

Repeat these 4 rows 9[8, 7, 6] times more. 100[135, 142, 134] sts.

Work *Decrease Row 1*.

P 1 row, working colors as set.

Repeat these 2 rows 0[4, 5, 4] times more.

When working the last of these Decrease Rows, work decreases as follows:

Using MC [k to 3 sts before color change, k2tog, ssk, k2tog, ssk] twice, k to end. 92[95, 94, 94] MC sts rem. Break CC yarn.

HOOD

Using MC, cont in St st for 10[10, 10.5, 10.5] inches, ending with a RS[WS, RS, RS] row.

Size 1X only:

Next Row [RS]: K47, k2tog, k to end.

All sizes:

Slip 46[47, 47, 47] sts to spare circular needle. Fold Hood in half with right sides together and join top seam of hood using a Three-Needle Bind Off.

Edging:

Using US #8/5mm needle and with WS facing, pick up and p 3 sts in every 4 rows along front edges of sweater, beg at lower left corner and working up left front, around, hood, and down right front. Work applied i-cord as described in Pattern Notes.

Finishing

Join Lower Body to Sleeves at under-arms using either Kitchener Stitch or Three-Needle Bind Off.

Weave in all ends.

Block, and sew in zipper.

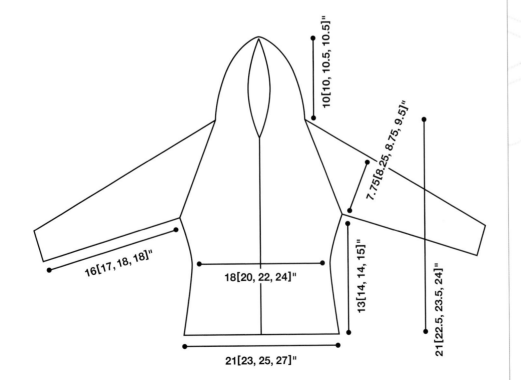

16[17, 18, 18]"

18[20, 22, 24]"

21[23, 25, 27]"

13[14, 14, 15]"

7.75[8.25, 8.75, 9.5]"

10[10, 10.5, 10.5]"

21[22.5, 23.5, 24]"

SIZE
L[1X, 2X, 3X]

FINISHED MEASUREMENTS
[in inches]
Bust: 43[47, 51, 59] closed
Hip: 48[52, 56, 64] closed
Sleeve at bicep: 14.5[14.5, 18, 18]
Length: 29.5[30, 30.5, 30.5]

MATERIALS
[MC] White Lies Designs Mojo
[78% mohair, 13% wool,
9% nylon; 100 yds/90 m per
50g skein]; color: Brunette;
10[11, 12, 14] skeins

[CC] White Lies Designs Joy
[100% merino wool; 100 yds/
90 m per 50g skein]; color:
Scarlet; 1 skein

1 29-inch US #11/8mm
circular needle

1 29-inch US #13/9mm
circular needle

Stitch holders

Tapestry needle

GAUGE
12 sts/16 rows =
4 inches in St stitch on smaller
needles in MC

Chocolate-Covered Cherry Jacket

by Joan McGowan-Michael

THIS DRAMATIC JACKET could have been too much of a good thing, but it's not. That's because it's knit in lace with delicate mohair yarn, so instead of overheating, you'll just look hot. It's coverage without overage. The short-row boob shaping accommodates your girls without bulking up the whole garment. The below-booty hem gives the smooth line you want if you've got junk in the trunk, and bell sleeves balance big upper arms.

Pattern

JACKET

Using larger needle and MC,
CO 145[157, 169, 193] sts.
K 4 rows.

Using CC, k 2 rows.
Using MC, work 4 rows in Lace pattern.
Repeat these 6 rows twice more.

Cont in Lace pattern until work measures 15 inches.

Using smaller needle, cont in Lace patt until work measures 18 inches, ending with a WS row.

Next Row [RS]: K8[7, 6, 11], k2tog, [k7[8, 9, 10], k2tog] 14 times, k to end. 130[142, 154, 178] sts rem.
P 1 row.

Optional bust shaping

If you wear a C cup or larger, you may wish to add short rows for bust shaping, as described below. All sizes start at C cup; D and larger continue with the next step, DD continue with the following step. If you wear larger than a DD cup, you may wish to work further short rows, decreasing the length of each pair of short rows by 1 st.
Each pair of short rows will add 0.5 inch to the length of the jacket front.

C cup:

K30[33, 36, 40], W&T, p to end.
K29[32, 35, 39], W&T, p to end.
K28[31, 34, 38], W&T, p to end.

D cup:

K27[30, 33, 37], W&T, p to end.

Pattern Notes

The body of this jacket is worked in one piece to the armholes, then it is divided and fronts and back are worked separately.

LACE PATTERN (Worked over a multiple of 12 sts + 1):
Row 1 [RS]: K1, [k2tog, k2tog, (YO, k1) 3 times, YO, ssk, ssk, k1] to end.
Row 2 [WS]: K all sts.
Repeat these 2 rows for Lace pattern.

TIPS FOR MAKING MOHAIR BEHAVE: Mohair yarn can be sticky to knit with. If you find yourself fighting with your mohair and you're using wooden or plastic needles, switch to aluminum: the mohair will slide right along.

If you think you've made a mistake in your mohair project, rip it out right away. Don't wait to see if it looks okay. Ripping back more than a couple of rows of mohair knitting is so frustrating, you'll be ripping out your hair, too.

DD cup:
K26[29, 32, 36], W&T, p to end.

All sizes:
K to end of row. When you encounter a wrapped st, pick up the wrap and place it on the left needle, then k it tog with the wrapped st.

C cup:
P30[33, 36, 40], W&T, k to end.
P29[32, 35, 39], W&T, k to end.
P28[31, 34, 38], W&T, k to end.

D cup:
P27[30, 33, 37], W&T, k to end.

DD cup:
P26[29, 32, 36], W&T, k to end.

All sizes:
P to end of row. When you encounter a wrapped st, pick up the wrap and place it on the left needle, then p it tog with the wrapped st.

After bust shaping is completed, work in St st until work measures 21 inches, ending with a WS row.
IMPORTANT: Measure length at back of jacket if short rows have been worked.

Shape armholes
Next Row [RS]: K26[27, 28, 32], BO 14[18, 22, 26] sts, k50[52, 54, 62], BO 14[18, 22, 26] sts, k26[27, 28, 32].
Next Row [WS]: P26[27, 28, 32], place rem sts on st holders.
Work in St st until work measures 8.5[8.5, 10, 10] inches from armhole BO, ending with a WS row.

Next Row [RS]: BO 12[13, 14, 16] sts, place rem 14[14, 14, 16] sts on st holder. With RS facing, rejoin yarn to Right Front. Work in St st until piece measures 8.5[8.5, 10, 10] inches from armhole BO, ending with a RS row.

Next Row [WS]: BO 12[13, 14, 16] sts, place rem 14[14, 14, 16] sts on st holder. With RS facing, rejoin yarn to back. Work in St st until work measures 8.5[8.5, 10, 10] inches from armhole BO.

BO 12[13, 14, 16] sts at beg of next 2 rows, BO rem 26[26, 26, 30] sts on foll row.

HOOD
Remove held sts from right front and place on needle with RS facing, k these sts, pick up and k 1 st in each of the 26[26, 26, 30] bound off sts at back neck, place held sts from left front on needle with RS facing and k these sts. 54[54, 54, 62] sts on needle.
Work 3 rows in St st.

Next Row [RS]: K4, m1, [k5[5, 5, 6], m1] 9 times, k to end. 64[64, 64, 72] sts. Work in St st until work measures 13 inches from shoulder, ending with a WS row.

Shape right side of hood
Row 1 [RS]: K 32[32, 32, 36], place rem sts on holder.
Row 2 [WS]: P1, p2tog tbl, p to end.
Row 3 [RS]: K to last 3 sts, ssk, k1.
Repeat *Rows 2 and 3* once more, then repeat *Row 2* once more.
BO rem 27[27, 27, 31] sts.

Shape left side of hood
Replace held sts. on needle with RS facing, and rejoin yarn to center back of hood. *Row 1* [RS]: K all sts.
Row 2 [WS]: P to last 3 sts, p2tog.
Row 3 [RS]: K1, k2tog, k to end.
Repeat *Rows 2 and 3* once more, then repeat *Row 2* once more.
BO rem 27[27, 27, 31] sts.

SLEEVES (MAKE 2)
Using larger needle and MC, CO 49[49, 61, 61] sts.
K 4 rows.
Using CC, k 2 rows.

Using MC, work 4 rows in Lace pattern. Repeat these 6 rows twice more.

Cont in Lace Pattern until work measures 8 inches.

Using smaller needle, cont in Lace patt until work measures 17[17, 18, 18] inches, ending with a WS row.

Next Row [RS]: K5[5, 2, 2], k2tog, [k7, k2tog] 4[4, 6, 6] times, k to end. 44[44, 54, 54] sts rem.
Cont in St st until work measures 21[23, 23.5, 25] inches, ending with a WS row.

BO 2[2, 3, 3] sts at beg of next 6 rows.
BO 3[3, 4, 4] sts at beg of next 4 rows.
BO 5 sts at beg of next 2 rows.
BO rem 10 sts.

Finishing

Sew shoulder seams.
Sew sleeves into armholes as follows:
sew curved, bound-off edge of sleeve
cap to vertical edge of armhole, then
sew top 2[3, 3.75, 4.25] inches of sleeve
to bound off edge of armhole.
Sew sleeve seams.
Sew hood seam.

EDGING

Using smaller needle and MC, with
RS facing and beginning at lower right
corner of front, pick up and k 3 sts for
every 4 rows along right front edge,
around edge of hood, and along left
front edge.

*In order to work the lace pattern for the
edging, it is important to have a multiple
of 12 sts + 1 (for example, the sample
shown has 193 sts) so increase or decrease
sts as necessary evenly over this next row to
attain an appropriate number of sts. The
short row bust-shaping options affect the
final number of rows worked at the front
edge, so you may end up with a different
number of picked-up stitches than we did.*
P 1 row.
Work 2 rows in Lace Pattern.
Using CC, k 2 rows.
Using MC, k 4 rows.
BO all sts loosely.
Steam garment lightly.

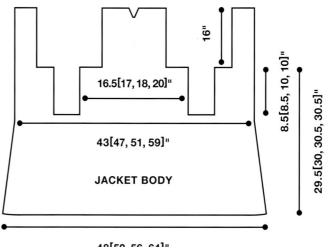

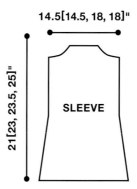

chapter 7

Bombshell

Boobalicious Tank

Cherry Bomb

Tanks and Tees

Laura Tee

SIZE
L[1X, 1.5X, 2X, 2.5X, 3X]

FINISHED MEASUREMENTS
[in inches]
Chest: 42[44, 46, 48, 50, 52]
Length: 20.5[21, 21.5, 22, 22.5, 23]

MATERIALS
Lorna's Laces Lion & Lamb
[50% silk, 50% wool; 205 yds/
184 m per 100g skein]; color:
Cedar; 4[4, 4, 5, 5, 6] skeins

1 24-inch US #8/5mm
circular needle

1 24-inch US #3/3.25mm
circular needle

Stitch markers

Safety pins or other removable
markers

Waste yarn

Tapestry needle

GAUGE
18 sts/24 rows = 4 inches in St
stitch using US #8/5mm needle

Bombshell

by Stefanie Japel

INSPIRED BY 1940's PINUP ART, Bombshell has a deep, squared-scoop neckline, inverted V bodice detail, and a nipped-in silhouette. The ribbing creates or defines a waist—whichever you need. The raglan sleeves balance your top and the fit-and-flare shape balances the rest of you. In fact, this fitted sweater flatters any figure. Oh yeah? Yeah. We tried it on all the models in this book and every single one of them looked amazing. If you like things smooth, wear it with the knit side out. Like a little texture? Then the purl side is for you.

Pattern

YOKE
Using larger needle, CO 66 sts.
Set-up Row [RS]: Kfb, place marker, kfb, k12, kfb, place marker, kfb, k34, kfb, place marker, kfb, k12, kfb, place marker, kfb. 74 sts.

Next Row [WS]: Sl 1 pwise, p to end.
Next Row [RS]: Sl1, [k to last st before marker, kfb, kfb] 4 times, k to end. Repeat these 2 rows 21 times more. 250 sts.

CO 34 sts using backward loop method. 284 sts. Place marker and join to begin working in the round, being careful not to twist new CO edge.

Next Round: K all sts.
Next Round: [K to 1 st before marker, kfb, kfb] 4 times, k to end.
Repeat these 2 rounds 6[8, 10, 12, 14, 16] times more. 340[356, 372, 388, 404, 420] sts on needle; 96[100, 104, 108, 112, 116] sts in larger sections, 74[78, 82, 86, 90, 94] sts in smaller sections.

The smaller sections of the yoke form the raglan sleeve caps, and the larger sections form the upper front and back of the top (the front is the section with the deep square neckline).

Try it on!
• *Slip Sleeve sts, Front sts and Back sts to separate pieces of waste yarn (in preparation for next step). Pin yoke together at under-arms and try on. Do the sleeves meet at the underarms? If there is too much extra fabric, the sweater is too big, and you should rip back a few rows. If the yoke is too small, work a few rounds extra; consider making a larger size.* •

LOWER BODY
Leaving Sleeve sts on waste yarn, replace

2

Pattern Notes

This top is worked from the top down. This method of knitting provides many opportunities for custom fitting, and offers the advantage of allowing you to try on your work at every stage. At various points in the pattern, suggestions are given for ways to customize the fit of this top. These suggestions are marked with bullets (•).

SEED STITCH (Worked in the round OR back and forth, over an even number of sts):
Row or Round 1: [K1, p1] to end.
Row or Round 2: [P1, k1] to end.

W3TOG: Work next 3 sts tog in patt.
(If the next st is a p st, p3tog. If the next st is a k st, k3tog.)

Back and Front sts on needle and join to begin working lower body in the round. Work to point where Back meets Front under right arm and place marker — this will now be the beginning of each round. 192[200, 208, 216, 224, 232] sts on needle.

K 4 rounds.

Place back darts

Set-up Round: K126[132, 138, 144, 150, 156], place marker, k36, place marker, k30[32, 34, 36, 38, 40].

Next Round: K to 2 sts before marker, ssk, k to next marker, k2tog, k to end.
Next Round: K all sts.
Repeat these 2 rounds 2 times more.

If you wish to work short rows for more length in the bust area, work them now. See Chapter 4 for notes on working short rows.

Place front darts and center rib patt

While Back Darts are worked every <u>other</u> round, Front Darts are worked every round.

Set-up Round: K28[30, 32, 34, 36, 38], ssk, place marker, k36, place marker, k2tog, k to 2 sts before third marker, ssk, k to fourth marker, k2tog, k to end.

Next Round: K to 2 sts before first marker, ssk, k17, p2, k17, k2tog, k to end.
Next Round: K to 2 sts before first marker, ssk, k17, p2, k17, k2tog, k to 2 sts before third marker, ssk, k to fourth marker, k2tog, k to end.
Repeat these 2 rounds once more.

Next Round: K to 2 sts before first marker, ssk, k13, [p2, k2] twice, p2, k13, k2tog, k to end.
Next Round: K to 2 sts before first marker, ssk, k13, [p2, k2] twice, p2, k13, k2tog, k to 2 sts before third marker, ssk, k to fourth marker, k2tog, k to end.
Repeat these 2 rounds once more.

Next Round: K to 2 sts before first marker, ssk, k9, [p2, k2] four times, p2, k9, k2tog, k to end.
Next Round: K to 2 sts before first marker, ssk, k9, [p2, k2] four times, p2, k9, k2tog, k to 2 sts before third marker, ssk, k to fourth marker, k2tog, k to end. 152[160, 168, 176, 184, 192] sts rem.
Work 2 rounds in patt as set with no further decreases.

• As written, the waist measurement of this top is approx. 9 inches smaller than the bust measurement. Every pair of decreases worked reduces the circumference of the top by slightly less than half an inch.

If you want to reduce the circumference at the waist more than is written, work more rounds of dart decreases; if you want the waist to taper less, work fewer rounds of dart decreases.

If you are working fewer rounds of dart decreases, it is still important to reach the same length before the ribbed waistband as if you were working all the rounds of dart decreases written. Consider working one plain knit round between the pairs of dart decrease rounds, or working a few extra rounds before beginning your darts. The solution you choose will depend on how many decrease rounds you choose to work. The pattern as written has 24 rounds worked below the underarms—be sure you have at least this many rounds. •

Next Round: Keeping st markers in place and using smaller needles, work in k2, p2 ribbing beg with 2 p sts[2 k sts, 2 p sts, 2 k sts, 2 p sts, 2 k sts]. *Ribbed detail at center front should line up with new ribbing.* Work 25 more rows in k2, p2 ribbing.

Shape hip

Next Round: Using larger needle, k all sts.
Next Round: [K to 1 st before marker, kfb, k to marker, kfb] twice, k to end.
Repeat these 2 rounds 5[5, 5, 6, 6, 6] times more. 176[184, 192, 204, 212, 220] sts.

• At this point, transfer all sts to waste yarn and try on top. Is it long enough?

How is the fit at the hip? There's only about one more inch left to go on the body, so determine whether you want your top to be longer, shorter, wider or narrower.

If the top flares too much, rip back to the rib and work fewer increase rounds—perhaps work 2 knit rounds between them instead of one, and only work 3 or 4 increase rounds.

If the top doesn't flare enough, either work more increase rounds or, if necessary, rip back to the rib and work 2 increase rounds in a row, then 1 plain knit round—do this a couple of times before working increases every other round as written.

If you are going to lengthen your top from this point, do you need to work more increase rows, or work straight? Observe the shape of your hips below where the top currently ends, and determine whether more increase rows will be necessary.•

Work 7 rounds of Seed stitch.
BO all sts loosely in patt.

SLEEVE BORDER
(WORK ON BOTH SLEEVES)

Transfer Sleeve sts to smaller needle. Rejoin yarn and work 9 rows in Seed stitch, back and forth. BO loosely in patt.

NECKLINE BORDER

With RS facing, using smaller needle and beg at right back corner, pick up and k 1 st in corner, 34 sts along back neck, 1 st in corner, 14 sts along top of left sleeve, 32 sts (or 3 sts for every 4 rows) down left front neckline, 1 st in corner, 34 sts along front neckline, 1 st in corner, 32 sts (or 3 sts for every 4 rows) up right front neckline, 14 sts along top of right sleeve. 164 sts. *(It is all right if this number does not match your number if you have picked up a different number of sts along right and left front neck edges; just be sure the number of sts you have picked up is the same on both sides.)*
Place safety pins or other removable markers in each corner st.

Work 2 rounds in Seed stitch.

Next Round: [Work in patt as set to 1 st before corner st, w3tog] 4 times. *The last w3tog will encroach on the beginning of the next round.*
Repeat these 3 rounds once more.
148 sts. BO all sts loosely in patt.

Finishing

Sew Sleeve Borders together at underarms. Weave in ends. Block as desired.

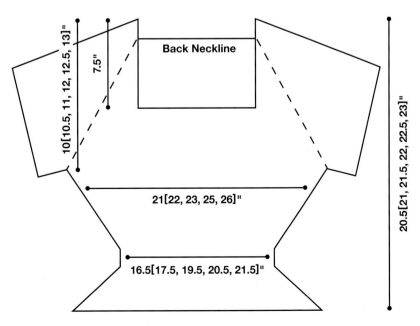

SIZE
L[1X, 2X, 3X]

FINISHED MEASUREMENTS
[in inches]
Chest: 43[46, 49, 52]
Hips: 51[54, 57, 60]
Length: 25

MATERIALS
Dale of Norway Svale (50%
cotton, 40% viscose, 10% silk;
114 yds/102 m per 50g ball);
color: 5582 Indigo; 10[11, 12,
13] balls

1 set US #5/3.75mm needles

Stitch markers

Stitch holders

Tapestry needle

GAUGE
22 sts/28 rows to 4 inches
in St stitch

Boobalicious Tank

by Amy M. Swenson

CALLING ALL BIG GIRLS: this tank is for you. The plunging V neck highlights your boobs, no matter how small or large they may be. It draws the eye up to balance a generous belly or butt (or both!). The waist is shaped, but not snug, so it suits belly girls. And if you've got booty, the extra ease at the hips will work for you.

Pattern

FRONT

*CO 140[150, 160, 170] sts.
Work 10 rows of Seed stitch.

Next Row [RS]: K45[50, 55, 60], place marker, work 50 sts in Seed stitch, place marker, k to end.
Next Row [WS]: P to marker, work 50 sts in Seed stitch, p to end.

Decrease Row [RS]: K to marker, k2tog, work in Seed stitch to 2 sts before marker, ssk, k to end.
Work 3 rows in patt as set.
Repeat these 4 rows 12 times more, then work *Decrease Row* once more.
112[122, 132, 142] sts rem.*

Panel shaping, Part 1

Row 1 [WS]: P6[11, 16, 21], place marker, p to marker, work in Seed stitch to marker, p to last 6[11, 16, 21] sts, place marker, p to end.
Row 2 [RS]: K1, m1, work in Seed stitch to marker, k to 2 sts before marker, ssk, work in Seed stitch to next marker, k2tog, k to marker, work in

Seed stitch to last st, m1, k1.
Row 3 [WS]: Work all sts in patt as set.
Row 4 [RS]: K1, m1, work in Seed stitch to marker, m1, slip marker, k to 2 sts before marker, ssk, k2tog, work in Seed stitch to 2 sts before marker, ssk, k2tog, k to 2 sts before marker, slip marker, m1, work in Seed stitch to last st, m1, k1.
Row 5 [WS]: Work all sts in patt as set.
Repeat *Rows 2–5* 4 times more.

Panel shaping, Part 2

Row 1 [RS]: K1, m1, work in Seed stitch to marker, m1, slip marker, k2tog, k to 2 sts before next marker, ssk, work in Seed stitch to next marker, k2tog, k to 2 sts before next marker, ssk, slip marker, m1, work in Seed stitch to last st, m1, k1.
Row 2 [WS]: Work all sts in patt as set.
Row 3 [RS]: K1, m1, work in Seed stitch to marker, m1, slip marker, k2tog, k to 2 sts before marker, ssk, k2tog, work in Seed stitch to 2 sts before marker, ssk, k2tog, k to 2 sts before marker, ssk, slip marker, m1, work in

Pattern Notes

To increase the length of this design, add additional rows of Moss stitch edging at the cast on edge, or in the Stockinette stitch and Seed stitch panels before beginning the shaping.

SEED STITCH (Worked over an even number of sts):
Row 1 [RS]: [K1, p1] to end.
Row 2 [WS]: [P1, k1] to end.
Repeat these 2 rows for Seed Stitch.

Seed stitch to last st, m1, k1.
Row 4 [WS]: Work all sts in patt as set.
Repeat these 4 rows 4 times more.
Remove center markers on last row
(leave side markers).
102[112, 122, 132] sts rem.

Bust shaping
Row 1 [RS]: Work in Seed stitch to
marker, m1, slip marker, k2tog, k6, ssk,
k2tog, k6, ssk, slip marker, m1, work in
Seed stitch to end.
Row 2 [WS]: Work in patt as set.
100[110, 120, 130] sts.

Row 3 [RS]: Work in Seed stitch to
marker, m1, slip marker, k2tog, k to 2
sts before marker, ssk, slip marker, m1,
work in Seed stitch to end.
Row 4 [WS]: Work in Seed stitch to
marker, m1, slip marker, p2tog tbl, p to
2 sts before marker, p2tog, slip marker,
m1, work in Seed stitch to end.
Repeat *Rows 3 and 4* 3 times more.
Remove markers on last row.

Work 2 rows in Seed stitch.

Shape armholes and neckline
BO 7[7, 9, 11] sts at beg of next 2
rows. 86[96, 102, 108] sts rem.
BO 2[3, 4, 5] sts at beg of next 2 rows.
82[90, 94, 98] sts rem.

Left armhole and neckline shaping
Row 1 [RS]: K2tog, work 37[41, 43,
45] sts in Seed stitch, ssk, place rem
41[45, 47, 49] sts on st holder.

Row 2 [WS]: Work all sts in Seed stitch.
Row 3 [RS]: K2tog, work to last 2 sts in
Seed stitch, ssk.
Repeat *Rows 2 and 3* 1[3, 4, 5] times
more. 35 sts rem.

Next Row [WS]: Work all sts in
Seed stitch.
Next Row [RS]: Work to last 2 sts in
Seed stitch, ssk.
Repeat these 2 rows 9 times more.
25 sts rem.

Work 3 rows in Seed stitch.
Next Row [RS]: Work to last 2 sts in
Seed stitch, ssk.
Repeat these 4 rows 4 times more.
20 sts rem.

Cont in Seed stitch until armhole measures 8[8, 9, 9] inches from first BO row.
BO all sts.

Right armhole and neckline shaping
Replace held sts on needle with RS
facing, rejoin yarn.

Next Row [RS]: K2tog, work to last 2
sts in Seed stitch, ssk.
Next Row [WS]: Work all sts in Seed
stitch.
Repeat these 2 rows 2[4, 5, 6] times
more. 35 sts rem.

Next Row [RS]: Work to last 2 sts in
Seed stitch, ssk.
Work 3 rows in Seed stitch.
Repeat these 4 rows 4 times more.
20 sts rem.

Cont in Seed stitch until armhole measures 8[8, 9, 9] inches from first BO row.
BO all sts.

BACK
Work from CO to beg of Panel
Shaping, Part 1 as for Front.

Work 3 rows in Seed stitch.
Next Row [RS]: K1, k2tog, work in Seed stitch to last 3 sts, ssk, k1.
Repeat these 4 rows 5 times more. 100[110, 120, 130] sts rem.

Cont in Seed stitch until Back measures same as Front to armhole.
Work from "Shape Armholes and Neckline" as for Front.

Finishing

Sew Back to Front at shoulders and sides. Weave in ends. Block as desired.

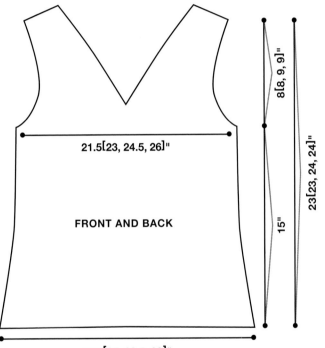

21.5[23, 24.5, 26]"

FRONT AND BACK

25.5[27, 28.5, 30]"

8[8, 9, 9]"

15"

23[23, 24, 24]"

SIZE
L[1X, 2X, 3X]

FINISHED MEASUREMENTS
[in inches]
Chest: 43[46.5, 51, 55]
Length: 24

MATERIALS
Lanaknits allhemp3 [100% long
fiber hemp; 150 yds/137 m per
45g skein]; color: 30 Cinnamon;
10[11, 12, 12] skeins

1 set 3mm needles,
24 inches or longer

1 set 3mm double-pointed
needles

*The metric 3mm needle is
between a US #2 and US #3 in
size. Use your discretion when
choosing your needle size.*

Tapestry needle

Stitch markers

Invisible zipper,
14 inches or longer

Sewing thread to match yarn

Sewing needle

2–3 yards ribbon or cord

GAUGE
28 sts/40 rows = 4 inches in St
stitch after blocking

Laura Tee

by Michelle Katerberg

THIS UNUSUAL TOP is flattering as anything for all Big Girls. Lacing at the shoulders adds interest, and you can adjust the sleeve length to show as much or as little arm as you like—just lace all the way to the end or don't lace much at all! The front gathers create vertical interest in the belly and boob area, which is delightful and distracting, and we know what the wrap does, right? It does it very well here. The fit is close to the body, but not tight. How do you get it on? It's got a side zip. Sexy.

Pattern

LEFT FRONT
CO 84 sts.
Rows 1 and 2: K.
Row 3 [RS]: K1, [YO, ssk] to last st, YO, k1. 85 sts.
Row 4: K.
Row 5 [RS]: K24, place marker, k to end. The stitches before the marker will be the drape sts.
Row 6: P.
Row 7 [RS]: Kfb in every st to marker, k to end of row. 109 sts; 48 drape sts.
Row 8: P.
Row 9 [RS]: K1, [kfb, k2] to 2 sts before marker, kfb, k1, k to last 4 sts, work Left Twist. 125 sts; 64 drape sts.
Work 7 rows in St st.

Shape neckline
Next Row [RS]: K to marker, slip marker, m1, k to last 4 sts, work Left Twist.

Work 3 rows in St st.
Next Row [RS]: K to marker, slip marker, m1, k to end.
Work 3 rows in St st.
Repeat these 8 rows 4 times more. 135 sts; 64 drape sts.

Next Row [RS]: K to marker, slip marker, m1, k28, kfb, place rem 42 sts on st holder for sleeve. 95 sts on needle.
P 1 row.

Sizes L and 1X only:
Next Row [RS]: K to marker, slip marker, m1, k to last 2 sts, m1, k2.
P 1 row.
Next Row [RS]: K to marker, slip marker, m1, k to end.
P 1 row.
Repeat these 4 rows 7 times more, working Left Twist every 8 rows as set. 119 sts.

Pattern Notes

This top is worked from the top down, and has some unusual construction details. The top right and left pieces (including the front halves of the cap sleeves) are cast on at the shoulder, and worked separately to just below the bust. They are joined, an extension is worked off the right front, and the lower front is worked down to the lower edge. The back is knit afterward.

In this pattern, there are garment sections that are knit with extra fullness, which will later be gathered and sewn into soft pleats for a draped effect. The stitches in these garment sections will be designated "drape sts."

As you work the short row sequences in this pattern, when you encounter a wrapped st, pick up the wrap, place it on your left needle, and work it together with the wrapped st. >>

CUSTOMIZATION NOTES:
If longer sleeves are desired, CO more sts for Left Front and Right Front. Make a note of how many extra sts are cast on, and add this number to the number of sts to place on hold for the sleeve. When casting on for the back, this number must be added twice to the CO, and once to every set of numbers in the Short-Row Neck Shaping sequence. (ie. If you have added 10 sts to each Front, add 20 sts when casting on the back, and add 10 sts to every number in the Short-Row Neck Shaping sequence.

The number of sts cast on at the end of the armhole shaping may also be altered to customize fit. Changing this number will change the full bust circumference. If this is done, be sure to change the number of rows knit in the last step when forming the sleeves as well; the inner edge of the sleeve will later be sewn to the curved edge and CO sts of the body under the arm.

RIGHT TWIST: K 4 sts onto double-point needle, rotate double-point needle 180 degrees counter clockwise, k sts from double-point needle onto working needle and continue working row.

LEFT TWIST: K last 4 sts onto double-point needle, rotate double-point needle 180 degrees clockwise, k sts from double-point onto working needle.

Sizes 2X and 3X only:
Next Row [RS]: K to marker, slip marker, m1, k to last 2 sts, m1, k2.
P 1 row.
Repeat these 2 rows 15 times more, working Left Twist every 8 rows as set. 127 sts.

All sizes:
Next Row [RS]: K to marker, slip marker, m1, k to end.

Next Row: P 1 row.

Repeat these 2 rows 13 times more. 138[144, 152, 159] sts.

Short-row bust shaping
If you have a very small bust, omit this section; instead, work as follows:
Next Row [RS]: k1[ssk, k2], 15 times, ssk, k1, remove marker, k to end.
P 1 row.
Resume pattern after Short-row bust shaping.

Row 1 [RS]: K1, [ssk, k2] 15 times, ssk, k1, remove marker, k19 [23, 23, 32], W&T.
Row 2: P12[14, 16, 18], W&T.
Each subsequent short row will be 6[6, 7, 7] sts longer than the last.
Row 3: K18[20, 23, 25], W&T.
Row 4: P24[26, 30, 32], W&T.
Row 5: K30[32, 37, 39], W&T.
Row 6: P36[38, 44, 46], W&T.
Row 7: K42[44, 51, 53], W&T.
Row 8: P48[50, 58, 60], W&T.
Row 9: K54[56, 65, 67], W&T.
Row 10: P60[62, 72, 74], W&T.
Row 11: K66[68, 79, 81], W&T.
Row 12: P72[74, 86, 88], W&T.
Row 13: K78[80, 93, 95], W&T.
Row 14: P84[86, 100, 102], W&T.
Row 15: K.
Row 16: P.
122[128, 136, 143] sts on needle.

This sequence adds approx. 1.5 inches of length over the left breast. For a very full bust, you may wish to work the sequence again as follows:
Next Row [RS]: K67[71, 76, 80], W&T. Repeat *Rows 2–16* again, for a total of 3 inches of added length.

All bust sizes resume shaping here
Next Row [RS]: K2tog 24 times, [k3[4, 4, 5], k2tog] 11 times, k rem 19[14, 22, 18] sts. 87[93, 101, 108] sts rem. Place all sts on st holder.

LEFT FRONT SLEEVE
Place held Sleeve sts on needle with RS facing, and rejoin yarn.
Row 1 [RS]: Kfb, k to last 4 sts, work Left Twist. 43 sts on needle.
Row 2: P 1 row.

Row 3 [RS]: K2, ssk, k to end.
Row 4 [WS]: P to last 4 sts, p2tog tbl, p2.
Repeat *Rows 3 and 4* 9[9, 10, 10] times more, working Left Twist at end of every 8th row as set. 23[23, 21, 21] sts rem.

Work 8[6, 16, 26] rows in St st, working Left Twist at end of every 8th row as set. BO all sts loosely.

RIGHT FRONT
CO 84 sts.
Rows 1 and 2: K.
Row 3 [RS]: K1, [YO, ssk] to last st, YO, k1. 85 sts.
Rows 4: K.
Row 5 [RS]: K61, place marker, k to end. The stitches after the marker will be the drape sts.
Rows 6: P.
Row 7 [RS]: K to marker, kfb in every st to end of row. 109 sts; 48 drape sts.
Rows 8: P.
Row 9 [RS]: Work Right Twist, k to marker, k1, [kfb, k2] to last 2 sts, kfb, k1. 125 sts; 64 drape sts.
Work 7 rows in St st.

Shape neckline
Next Row [RS]: Work Right Twist, k to marker, m1, slip marker, k to end.
Work 3 rows in St st.

Next Row [RS]: K to marker, m1, slip marker, k to end.
Work 3 rows in St st.
Repeat these 8 rows 4 times more. 135 sts.

Next Row [RS]: Work Right Twist, k37, kfb, place 43 sts just worked on st holder for sleeve, kfb, k to marker, m1, slip marker, k to end. 95 sts.
P 1 row.

Sizes L and 1X only:
Next Row [RS]: K2, m1, k ꞏ
m1, slip marker, k to enꞏ
P 1 row.
Next Row [RS]: K
marker, k to eꞏ
P 1 row.
Repeat ꞏ
workꞏ
1ꞏ

All siꞏꞏ
Row 1 [Rꞏ
marker, k to ꞏ
Row 2 [WS]: P tꞏ
17] sts. 127[130, 1ꞏ
Row 3 [RS]: K to markꞏ
marker, k to end.
Row 4: P.
Repeat these 2 rows 12 times more.
139[143, 151, 158] sts.

Next Row [RS]: K to marker, m1, slip marker, k1, [k2tog, k2] to last 3 sts, k2tog, k1. 122[128, 136, 143] sts rem.
P 1 row.

Short-row bust shaping
If you have a very small bust, omit this section; instead, work as follows:
Next Row [RS]: K to marker, m1, slip marker, k to end.

P 1 row.
Resume pattern after Short-row bust shaping.

Row 1 [RS]: K67[71, 76, 81], W&T.
Row ꞏ P12[14, 16, 18], W&T.
Eꞏ ꞏuent short row will be 6[6, 7, ꞏn the last.
ꞏ3, 25], W&T.
ꞏ2], W&T.
W&T.
ꞏT.

ꞏches of
a very full
ꞏ the sequence
ꞏ16 again, for a
ꞏdded length. If you do
ꞏ on the last RS row.

ꞏsizes resume shaping here
ꞏRow [RS]: K20[15,23,19], [K2
ꞏ5, K3[4, 4, 5] 11 times, place 64[70, 78, 85] sts just worked on st holder, k rem 48 sts.
P 1 row.
The remaining 48 sts will be worked later to form an extension, which will be gathered and sewn across the left side of the body, underneath the bust. At this point, the extension will be shaped using short rows, so that it will curve underneath the left breast without bulk.

Row 1: K12, W&T.
Row 2: P all sts.
Row 3: K24, W&T.
Row 4: P all sts.
Row 5: K36, W&T.

Row 6: P all sts.
Row 7: K all sts.
Row 8: P all sts.
Row 9: K8, W&T.
Row 10: P all sts.
Row 11: K16, W&T.
Row 12: P all sts.
Row 13: K24, W&T.
Row 14: P all sts.
Row 15: K32, W&T.
Row 16: P all sts.
Row 17: K40, W&T.
Row 18: P all sts.
Row 19: K all sts.
Row 20: P all sts.

Repeat Rows 1–12 once more.

RIGHT FRONT SLEEVE

Place held Sleeve sts on needle with WS facing, and rejoin yarn.
P 1 row.
Next Row [RS]: K to last 4 sts, k2tog, k2.
Next Row [WS]: P2, p2tog, p to end.
Repeat these 2 rows 9[9, 10, 10] times more, working Right Twist at beg of every 8th row as set. 23[23, 21, 21] sts rem.

Work 8[16, 16, 26] rows in St st, working Right Twist at beg of every 8th row as set. BO all sts loosely.

LOWER FRONT

Place held sts from both sides on circular needle with RS facing, so that center fronts are together. (DO NOT place 48 held drape sts from Right Front on needle—these remain on st holder.) Rejoin yarn.
Next Row [RS]: K to last st of Right Front, k last st of Right Front tog with first st of Left Front, k to end. 150[162, 178, 192] sts on needle.
Row 1: P.
Row 2 [RS]: K14[16, 16, 19], k2tog, k14[15, 16, 18], [k3[3, 4, 4], k2tog] 6 times, k9[11, 11, 13], k2tog, k8[10, 12, 12], k2tog, k9[11, 11, 13], [k2tog, k3[3, 4, 4]] 6 times, k14[15, 16, 18], k2tog, k14[16, 16, 19]. 134[146, 162, 176] sts rem.

Row 3 [WS]: [Sl 1, YO] to last st, sl1.
Row 4 [RS]: K1, [k2tog tbl] to end.
Repeat *Rows 3 and 4* once more.
Row 7 [WS]: P 55[61, 69, 76], place marker, p24, place marker, p 55[61, 69, 76]. *The sts between the markers will be the drape sts.*
Row 8 [RS]: [K11[12, 14, 15], m1] 4 times, k11[13, 13, 16], kfb 24 times, k11[13, 13, 16], [m1, k11[12, 14, 15]] 4 times. 166[178, 194, 208] sts.
Row 9: P.
Row 10 [RS]: K to marker, k1, [kfb, k2] 15 times, kfb, k1, k to end. 182[194, 210, 224] sts; 64 drape sts.

Shape waist

Work 7 rows in St st.
Next Row [RS]: K2, ssk, k to last 4 sts, k2tog, k2.
Repeat these 8 rows 5 times more. 170[182, 198, 212] sts.

Work 3 rows in St st.
Next Row [RS]: K3, m1, k to last 3 sts, m1, k3.
Repeat these 4 rows 9 times more. 190[202, 218, 232] sts.

Work 3 rows in St st.

Short-row hem shaping

Row 1: K to last 8[5, 4, 2] sts, W&T.
Row 2: P to last 8[5, 4, 2] sts, W&T.
[Note: Each subsequent short row will be 6[7, 8, 9] sts shorter than the last.]
Row 3: K to last 14[12, 12, 11] sts, W&T.
Row 4: P to last 14[12, 12, 11] sts, W&T.
Row 5: K to last 20[19, 20, 20] sts, W&T.
Row 6: P to last 20[19, 20, 20] sts, W&T.
Row 7: K to last 26[26, 28, 29] sts, W&T.
Row 8: P to last 26[26, 28, 29] sts, W&T.
Row 9: K to last 32[33, 36, 38] sts, W&T.
Row 10: P to last 32[33, 36, 38] sts, W&T.
Row 11: K to last 38[40, 44, 47] sts, W&T.
Row 12: P to last 38[40, 44, 47] sts, W&T.
Row 13: K to last 44[47, 52, 56] sts, W&T.

Row 14: P to last 44[47, 52, 56] sts, W&T.

Row 15: K to last 50[54, 60, 65] sts, W&T.

Row 16: P to last 50[54, 60, 65] sts, W&T.

Row 17: K to last 56[61, 68, 74] sts, W&T.

Row 18: P to last 56[61, 68, 74] sts, W&T.

Row 19: K to last 62[68, 76, 83] sts, W&T.

Row 20: P to last 62[68, 76, 83] sts, W&T.

Sts will be increased in the next row to ensure that the BO row will be long enough to allow the lower edge to curve gracefully.

Row 21: [K to wrapped st, m1, pick up wrap and place it on left needle, k wrap tog with wrapped st] 9 times, [k to wrapped st, pick up wrap and place it on left needle, k wrap tog with wrapped st, m1] 10 times, k to end.

Row 22: P to rem wraped st, pick up wrap and place it on left needle, p wrap tog with wrapped st, m1, p to end. BO all sts.

Place held sts from Right Front drape extension on needle, and k until extension is 0.5 inch short of reaching left side edge, ending with a WS row.

Next Row [RS]: [K3tog, ssk] to last 3 sts, k3tog. 19 sts rem.

K 5 rows. BO all sts loosely.

BACK
CO 210 sts.
K 2 rows.

Next Row [RS]: K1, [YO, ssk] 42 times, k40, [ssk, YO] 42 times, k1.
K 2 rows.

Short-row shoulder shaping
Row 1: P84, W&T.
Row 2: K.
Row 3: P86, W&T.
Row 4: K to last 4 sts, work Left Twist.
Row 5: P89, W&T.
Row 6: K.

Row 7: P93, W&T.
Row 8: K.
Row 9: P98, W&T.
Row 10: K.
Row 11: P.
Row 12: K 84, W&T.
Row 13: P.
Row 14: Work Right Twist, k82, W&T.
Row 15: P.
Row 16: K89, W&T.
Row 17: P.
Row 18: K93, W&T.
Row 19: P.
Row 20: K98, W&T.
Row 21: P.
Row 22: Work Right Twist, k to last 4 sts, work Left Twist.

Work 43 rows in St st, working Twists at each end of every 8th row as set.

Next Row [RS]: K41, kfb, place 43 sts just worked on st holder, kfb, k124, kfb, place rem 42 sts on st holder. 128 sts on needle.

Work 3[3, 1, 1] rows in St st.
Next Row [RS]: K2, m1, k to last 2 sts, m1, k2.
Repeat these 4[4, 2, 2] rows 7[7, 15, 15] times more. 144[144, 160, 160] sts.

P to end of row, CO 4[10, 10, 17] sts.
K to end of row, CO 4[10, 10, 17] sts.
152[164, 180, 194] sts.
Work 51 rows in St st.

Shape waist
Next Row [RS]: K2, ssk, k to last 4 sts, k2tog, k2.
Work 7 rows in St st.
Repeat these 8 rows 4 times more, then work first row (decrease row) once more. 140[152, 168, 182] sts.

Work 3 rows in St st.
Next Row [RS]: K3, m1, k to last 3 sts, m1, k3.
Repeat these 4 rows 9 times more. 160[172, 188, 202] sts.

Work 3 rows in St st.
Work Short-Row Hem Shaping and
BO as for Front.
Work Left Back Sleeve as for Right
Front Sleeve.
Work Right Back Sleeve as for Left
Front Sleeve.

Finishing

Wash pieces and lay flat to dry, flattening
sleeve, back neck and hem edges.
*Use doubled strand of matching-color
sewing thread to sew all seams, as yarn
may break if used for seaming.*
Sew Sleeves to Body at shaped underarm edges.
Sew right side and Sleeve seams.
Sew left sleeve seam and 0.5 inch of left
side seam. Baste rest of side seam closed.
Sew zipper into left seam with closed
end at underarm. The zipper will be
longer than the seam; fold the excess
length of zipper tape on each side and
sew securely under the zipper tape of

the working length of the zipper.
*Fabric may stretch lengthwise with wear,
in which case the lower portion of the zipper can be unsewn, and the extra length
of zipper tape can be used to lengthen the
zipper accordingly.*

Sew Back to Front at shoulders along
width of drape sts. (This seam can be
sewn longer if desired.)

Try on top and pin right front drape
extension to edge of left front, just in
front of zipper. Pin drape fabric into
soft pleats and folds. Take your time
with this, experiment with different
configurations. Use the photographs as a
starting point, but remember that this is
a good opportunity to make the garment
suit your body. When you are happy
with the look of the folds, sew them
securely in place from the wrong side
of the fabric.

Lace ribbon or cord through eyelets on
shoulders. If desired, sew ribbon or cord
over end of drape extension.

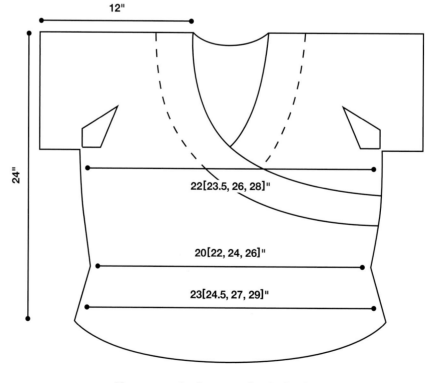

**Measurements shown are for the back piece.
Because of the draped sections of the front piece,
widths at the waist and hip may be adjusted.**

Cherry Bomb

by Joan McGowan-Michael

THE PERFECT PARTNER for the Chocolate-Covered Cherry (see page 86) is also gorgeous on its own. The deep square neckline shows some skin to keep your boobs visually separated and elongate your neck. It's nipped in at the waist and the short-row enhanced chest reduces the bulk so it's a great layering piece. But if you wear it alone, no worries—it's designed to cover bra straps. And the color? All eyes will be on you when you've got this on.

Pattern

FRONT
Using larger needle, CO 103[110, 115, 120, 125, 135, 145] sts.
K 4 rows.
Work in St st until work measures 3[3, 3.5, 3.5, 4, 4, 4] inches, ending with a WS row.

Waist shaping
Next Row [RS]: K1, k2tog, k to last 3 sts, ssk, k1.
Work 3 rows in St st.
Repeat these 4 rows 4 times more.
93[100, 105, 110, 115, 125, 135] sts rem.

Work 10 rows in St st.
Next Row [RS]: K1, m1, k to last st, m1, k1.
Work 5 rows in St st.
Repeat these 6 rows 4 times more.
103[110, 115, 120, 125, 135, 145] sts.

Short-row bust shaping
Use shaping if you wear a C cup or larger. See Pattern Notes at right.
Row 1: K to last 3 sts, W&T.
Row 2: P to last 3 sts, W&T.
Row 3: K to last 4 sts, W&T.
Row 4: P to last 4 sts, W&T.
Row 5: K to last 5 sts, W&T.
Row 6: P to last 5 sts, W&T.
Row 7: K to last 6 sts, W&T.
Row 8: P to last 6 sts, W&T.
Row 9: K to end of row. When you encounter a wrapped st, pick up the wrap and place it on the left needle, then k it tog with the wrapped st.
Row 10: P. Pick up each remaining wrap and p it tog with the wrapped st.

C cup: Work *Rows 1–10* once.
D cup: Work *Rows 1–10* twice.
DD cup: Work *Rows 1–10* three times.

Pattern Notes

SHORT-ROW BUST SHAPING
This shaping is recommended if you wear a C cup or larger. If you do not wish to work this shaping, continue working in St st until top is length indicated before armhole shaping. Similarly, if waist shaping is not desired, it can be omitted and the top worked straight in St st until work is length indicated before armhole shaping.

PESKY BRA STRAPS: This tank has great wide straps to hide your bra strap.

Still worried your bra will show? There are two great types of bra stap holders. One can be found in a lingerie store; it holds your bra straps together across your back. Another can be found in a sewing store; sew pieces of ribbon to the inside of your tank top to wrap around your bra strap and snap into place, out of sight.

SIZE
L[1X, 1.5X, 2X, 2.5X, 3X, 3.5X]

FINISHED MEASUREMENTS
[in inches]
Bust: 41[44, 46, 48, 50, 54, 58]
Length: 22[22, 22.5, 23, 23.5, 23.5, 24]

MATERIALS
White Lies Designs Joy [100% merino wool; 100 yds/90 m per 50g skein]; color: Scarlet; 7[7, 7, 8, 8, 8, 9, 9] skeins

1 set US #6/4mm needles

1 set US #4/3.75mm needles

Tapestry needle

GAUGE
20 sts/28 rows = 4 inches in St stitch using larger needles

All sizes:

Cont in St st until work (measured at side edge, outside short rows) measures 14[14, 14.5, 14.5, 15, 15, 15] inches, ending with a WS row.

Shape armholes

BO 7[7, 7, 8, 9, 11, 13] sts at beg of next 2 rows.

BO 5[5, 6, 7, 8, 10, 13] sts at beg of foll 2 rows.

Next Row [RS]: K1, k2tog, k to last 3 sts, ssk, k1.
P 1 row.
Repeat these 2 rows 2[2, 2, 3, 3, 3, 3] times more. 73[80, 83, 82, 83, 85, 85] sts rem.

Work 6 rows in St st.

Next Row [RS]: K12[14, 15, 14, 15, 16, 16], attach new ball of yarn, BO 49[52, 53, 54, 53, 53, 53] sts, k12[14, 15, 14, 15, 16, 16].
Work each side in St st until work measures 8[8, 8, 8.5, 8.5, 8.5, 9] inches from initial armhole BO.

BO all sts.

BACK

Using larger needle, CO 103[110, 115, 120, 125, 135, 145] sts.
K 4 rows.

Work in St st until work measures 3[3, 3.5, 3.5, 4, 4, 4] inches, ending with a WS row.

Waist shaping

Next Row [RS]: K1, k2tog, k to last 3 sts, ssk, k1.
Work 3 rows in St st.
Repeat these 4 rows 4 times more. 93[100, 105, 110, 115, 125, 135]sts rem.

Work 10 rows in St st.

Next Row [RS]: K1, m1, k to last st, m1, k1.
Work 5 rows in St st.
Repeat these 6 rows 4 times more. 103[110, 115, 120, 125, 135, 145] sts.

Cont in St st until work measures 14[14, 14.5, 14.5, 15, 15, 15] inches, ending with a WS row.

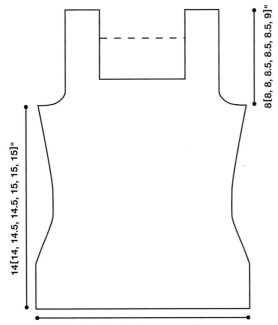

8[8, 8, 8.5, 8.5, 8.5, 9]"

14[14, 14.5, 14.5, 15, 15, 15]"

20.5[22, 23, 24, 25, 27, 29]"

Shape armholes

BO 7[7, 7, 8, 9, 11, 13] sts at beg of next 2 rows.
BO 5[5, 6, 7, 8, 10, 13] sts at beg of foll 2 rows.

Next Row [RS]: K1, k2tog, k to last 3 sts, ssk, k1.
P 1 row.
Repeat these 2 rows 2[2, 2, 3, 3, 3, 3] times more. 73[80, 83, 82, 83, 85, 85] sts rem.

Work 42 rows in St st.

Next Row [RS]: K12[14, 15, 14, 15, 16, 16], attach new ball of yarn, BO 49[52, 53, 54, 53, 53, 53] sts, k12[14, 15, 14, 15, 16, 16].
Work each side in St st until work measures 8[8, 8, 8.5, 8.5, 8.5, 9] inches from initial armhole BO.
BO all sts.

Finishing

Sew straps together at right shoulder. Using smaller needle, with RS facing and beg at left front shoulder, pick up and k 3 sts for every 4 rows, 1 st in each BO st, and 1 st in each corner around neckline.

Next Row [WS]: K.
Next Row [RS]: [K to 1 st before corner st, k3tog] 4 times, k to end.
Repeat these 2 rows once more.

BO all sts.
Sew straps together at left shoulder. Using smaller needle, with RS facing and beg at underarm, pick up and k 3 sts for every 4 rows and 1 st in each BO st around one armhole.
K 4 rows.
BO all sts.
Repeat for other armhole.
Sew side seams.
Weave in ends.
Block as desired.

chapter 8

Jackie Skirt

Yo! GaPants

Mosaic Skirt

Bottoms

Peel Skirt

Trinity Bay Skirt

SIZE
L[1X, 2X, 3X]

FINISHED MEASUREMENTS
[in inches]
Waist (before elastic insertion):
40.5[45.5, 50.5, 55]
Hips: 47[51, 56, 61]
Length: 25.5[25.5, 26, 26]

MATERIALS
Jo Sharp Silkroad DK Tweed
[85% wool, 10% silk, 5%
cashmere; 147 yds/135 m per
50g skein]

[MC] 405 Emporio; 7[7, 8, 9]
skeins

[CC] 406 Paper Rose; 3 skeins

1 set US #6/4mm needles

1 extra set US #6/4mm straight
or double-pointed needles

Small stitch holder

2 yards waistband elastic,
1 inch wide

Tapestry needle

GAUGE
20 sts/30 rows =
4 inches in St stitch

3

Jackie Skirt

by Jordana Paige

THIS SKIRT FEATURES the magical A-line shape, which looks good on every girl. And if you're a butt girl, read on. Look at that chevron…it's the key. It draws the eye down and away from where you might not want people focusing. It creates an interesting line that's totally *not* horizontal, and it visually balances whatever's above it. It also doesn't hit where your saddlebags might, if you have them.

Pattern

RIGHT FRONT

*Using MC, CO 53[59, 65, 71] sts.
Work in St st until work measures 1.25 inches, ending with a WS row.

Next Row [RS]: K24[27, 30, 33], [k into st below next st on left needle, and place this new st on a stitch holder, k next st] 5 times, k24[27, 30, 33].
Cont in St st until work measures 3 inches, ending with a WS row.

BELT LOOP

With RS facing, place held sts on extra needle and join a new ball of yarn.

Row 1 [RS]: K5.
Row 2 [WS]: K1, p3, k1.
Repeat these 2 rows until belt loop measures 1.75 inches, ending with a WS row. Break yarn.

Next Row [RS]: K24[27, 30, 33], [k next st tog with next st from belt loop] 5 times, k to end.

Next Row [WS]: P.*

Shape hips

Increase Row [RS]: K2, kfb, k to end.
Work 7 rows in St st.
Repeat these 8 rows 5 times more.
59[65, 71, 77] sts.

Work *Increase Row*. Work 9 rows in St st.
Repeat these 10 rows 3 times more, then work *Increase Row* once more.
64[70, 76, 82] sts.

Cont in St st until work measures 15.5 inches, or 11 inches less than desired length, ending with a RS row.

Work chevron pattern

See Pattern Notes for Decreasing Short Rows A, Chevron Stripe Rows A, and Increasing Short Rows A.
Next Row [WS]: P to last 3 sts, W&T.
K 1 row.

Pattern Notes

This skirt is worked from the waist down in four panels. The chevron pattern at the bottom is formed using short rows.

DECREASING SHORT ROWS A
Row 1 [WS]: P to 3 sts before last wrap, W&T.
Row 2 [RS]: K.
Row 3 [WS]: P to 2[—, 4, 4] sts before last wrap, W&T.
Row 4 [RS]: K.

CHEVRON STRIPE ROWS A
Row 1 [RS]: K to last 3 sts, kfb, k2.
Row 2 [WS]: P.

INCREASING SHORT ROWS A
Row 1 [RS]: K to wrapped st, pick up wrap and k wrap tog with wrapped st, k2, W&T.
Row 2 [WS]: P.
Row 3 [RS]: K to wrapped st, pick up wrap and k wrap tog with wrapped st, k3, W&T.
Row 4 [WS]: P. >>

DECREASING SHORT ROWS B
Row 1 [RS]: K to 3 sts before last wrap, W&T.
Row 2 [WS]: P.
Row 3 [RS]: K to 2[—, 4, 4] sts before last wrap, W&T.
Row 4 [WS]: P.

CHEVRON STRIPE ROWS B
Row 1 [RS]: K1, kfb, k to end.
Row 2 [WS]: P.

INCREASING SHORT ROWS B
Row 1 [WS]: P to wrapped st, pick up wrap and p wrap tog with wrapped st, p2, W&T.
Row 2 [RS]: K.
Row 3 [WS]: P to wrapped st, pick up wrap and p wrap tog with wrapped st, p3, W&T.
Row 4 [RS]: K.

Work *Decreasing Short Rows A* as follows:
Size L only: [Work *Rows 1–2* twice, work *Rows 3–4* once] 7 times.
Size 1X only: Work *Rows 1–2* 21 times.
Size 2X only: [Work *Rows 1–2* 4 times, work *Rows 3–4* once] 4 times, then work *Rows 1–2* twice more.
Size 3X only: Work *Rows 3-4* once, then work *Rows 1–4* 10 times.

All sizes:
Next Row [WS]: Using CC, p all sts. When you reach a wrapped st, pick up the wrap and place it on your left needle, then p it together with the wrapped st. Cont with CC, work *Chevron Stripe Rows A* 5 times. 69[75, 81, 87] sts.

Next Row [RS]: Using MC, k2, k2tog, k to last 3 sts, kfb, k2.
P 1 row.
Cont with MC, work *Chevron Stripe Rows A* 5 times. 74[80, 86, 92] sts.

Next Row [RS]: Using CC, k2, k2tog, k to last 3 sts, kfb, k2.
P 1 row.
Next Row [RS]: K4, W&T.
P to end.

Work *Increasing Short Rows A* as follows:
Size L only: Work *Rows 1–2* 22 times.
Size 1X only: [Work *Rows 1–2* 3 times, work *Rows 3–4* once] 5 times, then work *Rows 1-4* once.
Size 2X only: Work *Rows 1–4* 11 times.
Size 3X only: [Work *Rows 3–4* 3 times, work *Rows 1–2* once] 5 times, work *Rows 3–4* twice.

All sizes:
Next Row [RS]: K to wrapped st, pick up wrap and k wrap tog with wrapped st, k to end.
Work in St st until work measures 24.5[24.5, 25, 25] inches from top of belt loop.
Work in garter st for 1 inch.
BO all sts.

LEFT FRONT
Work as for Right Front from * to *.

Shape hips
Increase row [RS]: K to last 3 sts, kfb, k2.
Work 7 rows in St st.
Repeat these 8 rows 5 times more. 59[65, 71, 77] sts.

Work *Increase Row,* then work 9 rows in St st.
Repeat these 10 rows 3 times more, then work *Increase Row* once more. 64[70, 76, 82] sts.

Cont in St st until work measures 15.5 inches, or 11 inches less than desired length, ending with a WS row.

Work chevron pattern
See Pattern Notes for Decreasing Short Rows B, Chevron Stripe Rows B, and Increasing Short Rows B.

Next Row [RS]: K to last 3 sts, W&T.
P 1 row.

Work *Decreasing Short Rows B* as follows:
Size L only: [Work *Rows 1–2* twice, work *Rows 3–4* once] 7 times.
Size 1X only: Work *Rows 1–2* 21 times.
Size 2X only: [Work *Rows 1–2* 4 times, work *Rows 3–4* once] 4 times, then work *Rows 1–2* twice more.
Size 3X only: Work *Rows 3–4* once, then work *Rows 1–4* 10 times.

All sizes:
Next Row [RS]: Using CC, K all sts. When you reach a wrapped st, pick up the wrap and place it on your left needle, then k it together with the wrapped st.
P 1 row.
Cont with CC, work *Chevron Stripe Rows B* 5 times. 69[75, 81, 87] sts.

Next Row [RS]: Using MC, k1, kfb, k to last 4 sts, ssk, k2.
P 1 row.
Cont with MC, work *Chevron Stripe Rows B* 5 times. 74[80, 86, 92] sts.

Next Row [RS]: Using CC, k1, kfb,
k to last 4 sts, ssk, k2.
Next Row [WS]: P4, W&T.
K to end.

Work *Increasing Short Rows A* as follows:
Size L only: Work *Rows 1–2* 22 times.
Size 1X only: [Work *Rows 1–2* 3 times,
work *Rows 3–4* once] 5 times, then
work *Rows 1–4* once.
Size 2X only: Work *Rows 1–4* 11 times.
Size 3X only: [Work *Rows 3–4* 3 times,
work *Rows 1–2* once] 5 times, work
Rows 3–4 twice.

All sizes:
Next Row [WS]: P to wrapped st, pick
up wrap and k wrap tog with wrapped
st, p to end.
Work in St st until work measures
24.5[24.5, 25, 25] inches from top of
belt loop.

Work in garter st for 1 inch.
BO all sts.

BACK RIGHT
Work as for Left Front.

BACK LEFT
Work as for Right Front.

Finishing

Sew Right Front to Left Front at center,
so stripes form a V.
Repeat for Right Back and Left Back.
Sew Front and Back of skirt together at
sides. Weave in ends.
Fold top edge down 1.25 inches to inside
of skirt to form waistband casing. Sew
edge of casing to inside of skirt, leaving a
2-inch opening for elastic insertion.
Block skirt as desired.
Cut elastic piece one inch longer than
waist measurement. Insert elastic into
casing, being careful not to twist, and
sew ends together. Sew casing closed.
Weave in rem ends.

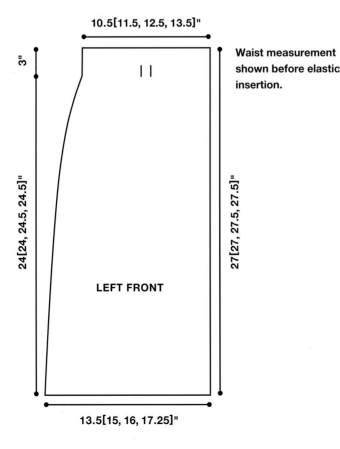

10.5[11.5, 12.5, 13.5]"

3"

**Waist measurement
shown before elastic
insertion.**

24[24, 24.5, 24.5]"

27[27, 27.5, 27.5]"

LEFT FRONT

13.5[15, 16, 17.25]"

SIZE
L[1X, 2X, 3X]

FINISHED MEASUREMENTS
[in inches]
Waist (before elastic insertion):
47.5[50.75, 54, 57.25]
Hip: 47.5[50.75, 54, 57.25]
Length: 40.5[41.25, 41.75, 42.5]
(can be adjusted to fit)

MATERIALS
Artful Yarns Candy [64% cotton,
32% acrylic, 3% nylon, 1%
elastic; 119 yds/107 m per 50g
skein]; color: 9367 Sour Apple;
17[19, 20, 22] balls

1 24-inch US #8/5mm
circular needle

1–1.5 yds of 1.5 inch soft waistband or sport elastic (depending
on desired waist measurement)

Crochet hook and waste yarn
(for provisional cast-on)

Stitch holders

Tapestry needle

GAUGE
20 sts/26 rows =
4 inches in St stitch

Yo! GaPants

by Alison Hansel

KNITTED PANTS aren't something everyone's considered making, but these are sinfully delicious. Besides, sometimes a yarn calls out and it must be listened to. In this case, the yarn is a cotton blend, and not only is it fun and sproingy, but it contains lycra. Which means you can knit stuff from it, sit down wearing that stuff, and watch the stuff spring back to shape when you stand up again. Good plan. These pants have flattering wide, straight legs that work for all types of butts. The ribbing down the side of the leg makes sure the pants stay looking like pants. You won't want to take them off.

Pattern

FRONT LEFT LEG
Using Crochet Cast On, CO 58[62, 66, 70] sts.
Row 1 [RS]: K to last 4 sts, p2, k2.
Row 2 [WS]: P all sts.
Work in patt as set until work measures 7[7.5, 8, 8] inches, ending with WS row.

Shape crotch
Increase Row [RS]: K2, m1, work in patt to end.
P 1 row.
Repeat these 2 rows 2[3, 3, 4] times more. 61[66, 70, 75] sts.

Next Row [RS]: Using knitted or cable method, CO 7[7, 8, 8] sts at the beginning of the next row, k these sts, work in patt to end of row. 68[73, 78, 83] sts.
Work 31 rows in patt as set.

Decrease Row [RS]: K2, k2tog, work in patt to end.
Work 19 rows in patt.
Repeat these 20 rows 8 times more. 59[64, 69, 74] sts rem.

Work in patt as set until work, from CO sts at crotch, measures 2 inches less than your inseam measurement, ending with a RS row.

Place rem sts on st holder or waste yarn.

FRONT RIGHT LEG
Using Crochet Cast On, CO 58[62, 66, 70] sts.
Row 1 [RS]: K2, p2, k to end.
Row 2 [WS]: P all sts.
Work in patt as set until work measures 7[7.5, 8, 8] inches, ending with WS row.

Pattern Notes

Pant legs are worked from the waist down, from a provisional Crochet Cast On. After all pieces have been worked and sewn together, the provisional cast on is removed and the waistband is worked in one piece from the resulting live sts.

INSEAM MEASUREMENT
This measurement is the length of the inside of your leg. Using a tape measure, standing straight, measure from your crotch to the floor. You will most likely need someone to help you with the floor end of the tape measure. >>

KNITTED CAST ON

Make a slip knot with just enough tail to weave in later, and place it on your L needle. That's stich #1. Knit into stitch #1 as usual, but instead of dropping the stitch off the L needle, pull the loop toward you with your R needle and slip it back on the end of the L needle, creating stitch #2.

Repeat, always using the newest stitch as the one you knit into, until you have as many stitches as desired on your L needle.

CABLE CAST ON

Start as for knitted cast on, creating 1 stitch, so you have 2 stitches on your L needle. Insert your R needle *between* the two stitches, wrapping and pulling a loop through as if you were knitting, and slip the loop back on the end of the L needle, creating stitch #3.

Repeat, always inserting your R needle between the two stitches closest to the tip of your L needle, until you have as many stitches as desired on your L needle.

Shape crotch

Increase Row [RS]: Work in patt to last 2 sts, m1, k2.
P 1 row.
Repeat these 2 rows 2[3, 3, 4] times more. 61[66, 70, 75] sts.

Next Row [RS]: Work in patt.
Next Row [WS]: Using knitted or cable method, CO 7[7, 8, 8] sts at the beg of the next row, p these sts, p to end of row. 68[73, 78, 83] sts.
Work 30 rows in patt as set.

Decrease Row [RS]: Work in patt to last 4 sts, ssk, k2.
Work 19 rows in patt.
Repeat these 20 rows 8 times more. 59[64, 69, 74] sts rem.

Work in patt as set until work, from CO sts at crotch, measures 2 inches less than your inseam measurement, ending with a RS row.

Place rem sts on st holder or waste yarn.

BACK LEFT LEG

Using Crochet Cast On,
CO 61[65, 69, 73] sts.

Row 1 [RS]: K3, p2, k to end.
Row 2 [WS]: P all sts.
Work in patt as set until work measures 7[7.5, 8, 8] inches, ending with WS row.

Shape crotch

Increase Row [RS]: Work in patt to last 2 sts, m1, k2.
P 1 row.
Repeat these 2 rows 5[6, 6, 7] times more. 67[72, 76, 81] sts.

Next Row [RS]: Work in patt.
Next Row [WS]: Using knitted or cable method, CO 7[7, 8, 8] sts at the beg of next row, p these sts, p to end of row. 74[79, 84, 89] sts.
Work 30 rows in patt as set.

Decrease Row [RS]: Work in patt to last 4 sts, ssk, k2.
Work 19 rows in patt.
Repeat these 20 rows 8 times more. 65[70, 75, 80] sts rem.

Work in patt as set until work, from CO sts at crotch, measures 3 inches less than your inseam measurement, ending with a RS row.

Place rem sts on st holder or waste yarn.

BACK RIGHT LEG

Using Crochet Cast On,
CO 61[65, 69, 73] sts.
Row 1 [RS]: K to last 5 sts, p2, k3.
Row 2 [WS]: P all sts.
Work in patt as set until work measures 7[7.5, 8, 8] inches, ending with WS row.

Shape crotch

Increase Row [RS]: K2, m1, work in patt to end.
P 1 row.
Repeat these 2 rows 5[6, 6, 7] times more. 67[72, 76, 81] sts.

Next Row [RS]: Using knitted or cable method, CO 7[7, 8, 8] sts at the beg of the next row, k these sts, work in patt to end of row. 74[79, 84, 89] sts.
Work 31 rows in patt as set.

Decrease Row [RS]: K2, k2tog,
work in patt to end.
Work 19 rows in patt.
Repeat these 20 rows 8 times more.
65[70, 75, 80] sts rem.

Work in patt as set until work, from
CO sts at crotch, measures 3 inches less
than your inseam measurement, ending
with a RS row.
Place rem sts on st holder or waste yarn.

Finishing

Using mattress st, sew Right Front and
Right Back pieces together at inseam
and side seam. Sew Left Front and Left
Back pieces together in the same way.
When sewing side seams, the back will
be about an inch longer than the front.
Distribute this ease between the waist
and the hip of the side seam.

Pin right and left halves together at tops
of inseams. Sew Fronts together from
inseam to waist, then sew Backs together
in the same way.

Remove crochet chains from CO and
place all live sts together on circular
needle. Beg at left side seam, k 1 round,
knitting 2 sts tog at each seam.
Work in the round in patt as set,
maintaining rib patt at side seams,
for 3 inches. BO all sts.

Cut a piece of waistband elastic 3
inches shorter than your actual waist
measurement. Overlap ends of elastic 1
inch and sew together, ensuring that
elastic is not twisted.
Place elastic inside waistband of pants
directly above first top of seams. Fold top
of waistband over elastic and sew edge of
waistband down to form elastic casing.
Place held sts of left leg on needle and k
1 round, knitting 2 sts tog at each seam.
Work in the round in patt as set, maintaining rib patt at side seam, for 2
inches. BO all sts.
Fold bottom inch of work to inside and
sew edge in place.
Repeat for right leg.
Weave in ends.

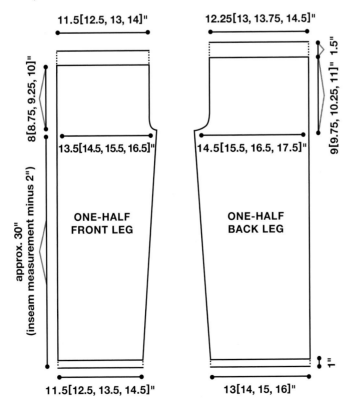

SIZE
L[1X, 2X, 3X]

FINISHED MEASUREMENTS
[in inches]
Hips: 44[48, 52, 56]

MATERIALS
Crystal Palace Mikado Ribbon
[50% rayon, 50% cotton;
112 yds/103 m per 50g skein]

[MC] 1809 Walnut;
10[11, 12, 13] skeins

[CC] Color: Bittersweet;
5[6, 6, 7] skeins

1 set US #9/5.5mm needles

1 24-inch or 32-inch
US #7/4.5mm circular needle

Waste yarn

Sewing thread, same color as MC

Sewing needle or machine

1 US I/5.5mm or US J/6mm
crochet hook

Safety pin or split ring markers

GAUGE
20 sts/24 rows =
4 inches in St stitch

Peel Skirt

by Rebecca Hatcher

KNIT IN RIBBON YARN, this inventive creation is perfect for Big Girls with shapely, generous booties. If you've got saddlebags you don't want noticed, though, this skirt isn't for you. Inspired by the skin of an orange, Peel starts in a point at the waist, and gets wider as it wraps around your body. After one wrap, the strip stops getting wider, ending with an asymmetrical hemline at any length you want. This unusual construction means that you can change the size once it's finished without reknitting the whole thing—just unravel the waistband, take out the seam, and wrap the strip into a narrower or wider tube. How's that for a custom fit?

Pattern

Using larger needles and MC, CO 5 sts.
Set-up Row 1 [RS]: Sl1, k1, place marker, p1, k2.
Set-up Row 2 [WS]: Sl1, p1, k1, p2.

Row 1 [RS]: Sl1, k to marker, m1, slip marker, p1, k2.
Rows 2 and 4 [WS]: Sl1, p1, k1, p to end.
Row 3 [RS]: Sl1, k to marker, p1, k2.
Repeat these 4 rows 64 times more. 70 sts.

Work *Rows 3 and 4* as above until work measures 102[114, 126, 138] inches from beg, measured along long straight edge.

Switch to CC, and cont in patt as set until work measures 144[156, 168, 180] inches, ending with a WS row. Place sts on waste yarn.

Finishing

Working on a large, flat surface with the right side out, beg at pointed end and wrap skirt into a flared tube shape, using schematic as a guide. The straight edge (without decreases) should be the upper edge of the skirt, and the lower edge (shaped edge with p rib) of each tier should overlap the upper edge of each subsequent tier slightly.
Sew edges of strip together beg at waist and ending 12–24 inches from end of strip. Use a double thickness of sewing thread and make small, closely spaced stitches. If you are comfortable using a sewing machine, a machine-sewn seam would be more durable. Pin rem length of strip in place and try on skirt to check length. If skirt is too long, unravel knitted fabric to desired length. If skirt is too short, knit to desired length.

Pattern Notes

Each additional skein of Mikado will add about 12 inches to the strip, giving you 4 more inches of width.

TIPS FOR WORKING WITH RIBBON
Ribbon yarn can become twisted while knitting with it, which is part of its charm. If you really don't like the look of twisted ribbon, the remedy is to untwist the ribbon after every couple rows of knitting.

Ribbon yarns are slippery and don't stay neatly in balls. To keep knitting smoothly and prevent the yarn from tangling, try a zip-top bag. Poke a small hole in the bottom of the bag, thread the yarn end through the hole, and seal the naughty ball of ribbon in the bag.

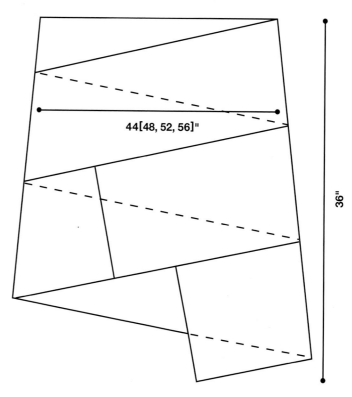

Some lengthwise stretching will occur with wear, so allow at least 3 inches for stretching when determining length.

Sew rem length of strip in place.

LOWER FACING

Place held sts on needle with RS facing and rejoin yarn.
P 1 row to form turning ridge.
Work 6 rows in St st, loosely BO all sts.
Fold facing to inside of skirt and sew in place.

WAIST FACING

Try on skirt again in front of a full-length mirror. Rotate it around your hips to determine the most pleasing place for the center front. Once you have determined this, mark it with a safety pin at the waist edge.
Using smaller needles and CC, beg at center front and with RS facing, pick up and k 144[164, 184, 204] sts around waist.
Work back and forth in St st for 4 rows, then join and work in the round in St for 4 rows.
BO all sts loosely.
Fold facing to inside and sew in place.

DRAWSTRING

Using MC or CC doubled, work a crochet chain at least twice as long as waist circumference of skirt. Insert into waist facing, with ends emerging from opening at center front.

44[48, 52, 56]"

36"

**These are only suggested, approximate measurements.
All measurements are adjustable.**

Trinity Bay Skirt

by Jodi Green

WHEN YOU KNIT A SKIRT, you should make a statement. This knitted skirt says that a) you can K.N.I.T. and b) you know how to dress yourself. Again it has the A-line shape, which we know flatters girls of all body shapes, especially those who've got low and generous butts. It also skims past saddlebags, thanks to the substantial-but-not-bulky yarn it's knit in. The slithering Celtic knotwork adds interest and distracts from any belly action you've got going on. And if you're feeling like it, add the optional cargo pocket wherever it suits you…at the knee or lower, to further balance your booty.

Pattern

CO 222[238, 252, 270, 286] sts.
Work in Seed st until work measures 1 inch, ending with a RS row.

Next Row [WS]: Work 9[7, 6, 9, 13] sts in patt, m1, [work 17[16, 15, 14, 13] sts in patt, m1] 12[14, 16, 18, 20] times, work rem 9[7, 6, 9, 13] sts in patt. 235[253, 269, 289, 307] sts on needle.
Next Row [RS]: Work 5 sts in Seed st as set, k 54[58, 62, 67, 72], place marker, k 49[54, 58, 63, 67], place marker, work Row 1 of Chart A, place marker, 49[54, 58, 63, 67], place marker, k 54[58, 62, 67, 72], work rem 5 sts in Seed st as set.
The first and fourth markers indicate placement of side "seams" and side shaping. The second and third markers indicate placement of the cable panel.

Read through all instructions before continuing; skirt shaping and cable shaping happen simultaneously.
Work cable panel as follows:
Work through Chart A once, then work through all rows of Chart B and repeat Chart B until waist shaping begins.
Once waist shaping has begun, work to Row 18 of Chart B, then work Chart C. Once all rows of Chart C have been worked, remove markers indicating cable panel placement and continue in St st.
12 sts are added when Chart A is worked. Once Chart A has been completed, there will be 247[265, 281, 301, 319] sts on needle.
AT THE SAME TIME: Continue in patt as set until work measures 3 inches ending with a WS row.

SIZE
L[1X, 2X, 3X, 4X]

FINISHED MEASUREMENTS
[in inches]
Waist (before elastic insertion):
34[38, 42, 46, 50]
Hip: 44[48, 52, 56, 60]
Length: 31[31.5, 32, 32.5, 33]
(not including 1-inch waistband)

MATERIALS
Jo Sharp Desert Garden Aran
Cotton [65% cotton, 35%
microfiber; 60 yds/55 m per
50g skein]; color: 241 Marina;
23[24, 26, 28, 30] skeins

1 32-inch US #8/5mm circular
needle (for larger sizes, a 40-
inch needle may be preferable)

1 cable needle

4 stitch markers if working
back and forth, 5 if working
in the round

1 piece of 1-inch waistband
elastic, 2 inches shorter than
waist measurement

1 piece interfacing or lightweight
buckram, 6 by 8 inches (optional)

2 buttons, 1 to 1.5 inch in
diameter (optional)

GAUGE
18 sts/24 rows =
4 inches in St stitch

Decrease Row [RS]: Work in patt as set to 2 sts before first marker, k2tog, ssk, work in patt as set to 2 sts before fourth marker, k2tog, ssk, cont in patt as set to end of row.

Work 13 rows in patt as set.

Repeat these 14 rows 8 times more. 211[229, 245, 265, 283] sts rem.

AT THE SAME TIME, when work measures 10 inches from top of Seed st border (or desired length of back slit):

If you prefer to work back and forth, inc 1 st beg and end of next row end and work for 6 more rows, maintaining Seed st borders and working new edge sts in St st. On 7th row, end Seed st borders and beg working these sts in St st (these sts will be worked in St st for the remainder of the skirt).

*All stitch counts from this point will **not** include the edge sts. Add 2 sts to st counts given.*

Alternatively, if you prefer to work in the round, do not increase sts. Join to begin working in the round, place marker to indicate beg of round, and continue to work the 10-st Seed st section in Seed St for 6 more rows; on 7th row knit across all these sts and cont working these sts in St st.

All knitters continue here

When side shaping is complete, cont in patt as set until work measures 25 inches from beg.

Shape waist

Work *Decrease Row* as above, then work 3 rows in patt as set.

Repeat these 4 rows 5[7, 10, 10, 10] times more.

Sizes L and 1X only:

Work *Decrease Row* as above, then work 1 row in patt as set.

Repeat these 2 rows 4[2] times more.

All sizes:

After Chart C has been worked and all waist shaping has been completed,

155[173, 189, 209, 227] sts rem.

Cont in St st until work measures 33.5[34, 34.5, 35, 35.5] inches from beg. BO all sts.

POCKET

CO 28 sts.

Work 5 rows in Seed st.

Next Row [WS]: Work 14 sts in patt as set, m1, work in patt as set to end.

Next Row [RS]: Work 5 sts in Seed st as set, work Row 1 of Chart A, Work rem 5 sts in Seed st as set.

Cont in patt as set, working through Chart A once, then through Rows 1–18 of Chart B once, then through Chart C once, maintaining 5-st Seed st borders.

Next Row [WS]: Work 14 sts in Seed st, dec 1 st in patt (if the next st is a k st, k2tog; if it is a p st, p2tog), cont in Seed st to end.

Work 5 more rows of Seed st.

BO all sts in patt.

OPTIONAL POCKET FLAP

CO 28 sts. Work 3 rows in Seed st.

Next Row [WS]: Work 3 sts in patt as set, BO 3 sts, work 16 sts in patt as set, BO 3 sts, work rem 3 sts in patt as set.

Next Row [RS]: Work 3 sts in patt as set, CO 3 sts, work 16 sts in patt as set, CO 3 sts, work rem 3 sts in patt as set.

Work 3 more rows in Seed st.

BO all sts in patt.

Finishing

Weave in ends.

Block lightly.

If skirt was worked back and forth, sew back seam above slit using mattress st. Fold top down 1.25 inches to inside of skirt to form waistband casing. Sew edge to inside of skirt, leaving a 2-inch

opening for elastic insertion. Insert elastic into casing, being careful not to twist, and sew ends together. Sew casing closed. If desired, cut a piece of interfacing or lightweight buckram slightly smaller than size of pocket and whipstitch it to inside of pocket.

Center pocket over line of side decreases at desired height and sew to skirt. Position pocket flap so that top edge of flap sits slightly above top edge of pocket and sew to skirt along top edge. Position buttons on pocket beneath buttonholes and sew into place. Weave in rem ends.

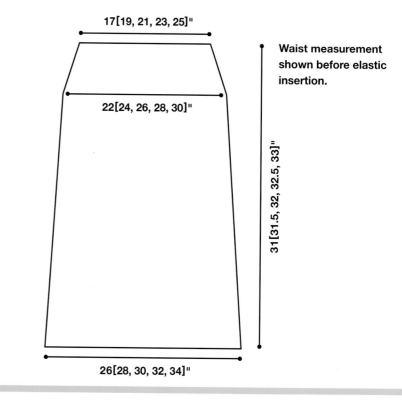

17[19, 21, 23, 25]"

22[24, 26, 28, 30]"

Waist measurement shown before elastic insertion.

31[31.5, 32, 32.5, 33]"

26[28, 30, 32, 34]"

KEY

■ (empty square) no stitch; adjacent increase sts will create a new st to fill this space in the next row

— p on RS, k on WS

| k on RS, p on WS

V [k1 tbl, k1] in st, insert needle in vertical strand between the 2 new sts, k this; makes 2 new sts

V [p1, yo, p1] in st on RS, [k1, p1, k1] in st on WS; makes 2 new sts

sl 2 sts to cn, hold to front, p1, k 2 from cn

sl 1 sts to cn, hold to back, k2, p1 from cn

sl 2 sts to cn, hold to front, p2, k2 from cn

sl 2 sts to cn, hold to back, k2, p2 from cn

sl 2 sts to cn, hold to front, k2, k2 from cn

sl 2 sts to cn, hold to back, k2, k2 from cn

sl 3 sts to cn, hold to back, k2, sl p st back to left needle and p it, k2 from cn

dec 5 sts to 1 thus: sl 3 kwise (one at a time), *pass 2nd st on right needle over first (center st), sl center st back to left needle, pass next st over*, sl center st back to right needle, rep * to *, p remaining (center) st

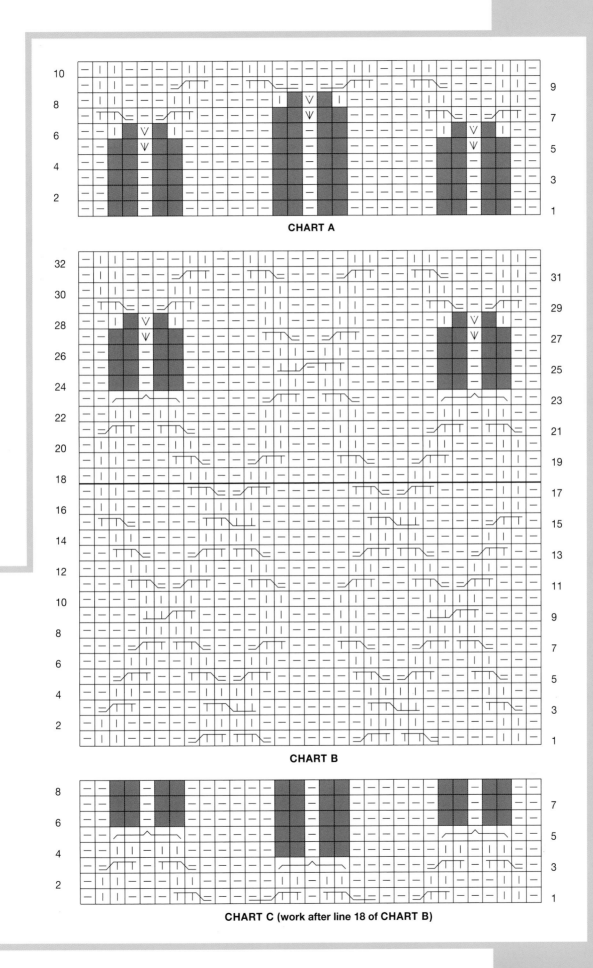

CHART A

CHART B

CHART C (work after line 18 of CHART B)

SIZE
L[1X, 2X, 3X]

FINISHED MEASUREMENTS
[in inches]
Hip circumference:
40[46, 52, 57]
Waist circumference:
32[37, 43, 48]
Skirt Length:
23[23, 24, 24]

MATERIALS
Cascade Pastaza [50% llama,
50% wool; 132 yds/119 m per
100g skein]

[MC] 010 Rust; 6[7, 8, 9] skeins

[CC] 077 Mustard; 1 skein

1 US #5/3.75mm circular needle,
36-inch for L and 1X, 40-inch for
2X and 3X

1 US #4/3.5mm circular needle,
24-inch or longer

1 spare US #4/3.5mm or smaller
circular needle, 24 inches or
longer, will be used to hold
stitches

Stitch markers

Tapestry needle

2 yards 1-inch wide waistband
elastic

GAUGE
20 sts/26 rows = 4 inches in St
stitch on larger needles

Mosaic Skirt

by Kristi Porter

THIS SLEEK SKIRT is just the thing to pair with the coordinating sweater (see page 54), or wear it with a fine-looking tailored blouse. It's a straight skirt, so it suits belly girls and girls with back-jutting butt. The mosaic design is saved only for the hem this time, so it's not too much on the bottom, where you may already have more than you'd like.

Pattern

MOSAIC BORDER

Using CC and US #4/3.5mm needles, CO 101[115 ,129, 143] sts.
K 1 row.
Join MC and work Rows 1–20 of Mosaic Pattern in garter stitch, using CC for Color A and MC for Color B.
K 2 rows using CC.
Place on hold on spare circular needle.

Make a second piece in the same way. Break CC.

When second piece is completed, k all sts using MC and US #5/3.75mm needle, then with RS facing, k all sts of held piece from spare needle to US #5/3.75mm needle, so both pieces are joined on one circular needle. Place marker and join to begin working in the round. 202[230, 258, 286] sts. Continue to work in St st until skirt measures 15[15, 16, 16] inches, or 8 inches less than desired length to waist.

Next Round: K15, place marker, k 71[85, 99, 113], place marker, k30, place marker, k 71[85, 99, 113], place marker, k to end.
Decrease Round: [K to marker, k2tog, k to 2 sts before next marker, ssk] twice, k to end.
K 3 rounds.
Repeat these 4 rounds 10 times more. 158 [186, 214, 242] sts rem.

Using US #4/3.5mm needle, work in k1, p1 rib for 2 inches. BO all sts loosely.

Finishing

Weave in ends. Block skirt.
Cut a length of elastic long enough to fit snugly but comfortably around your waist, plus 1 inch.
Overlap ends of elastic about 1 inch and sew together.
Position elastic inside ribbed waistband of skirt and stitch in place with overcasting.

Pattern Notes

Choose the size that best fits your hip measurement. Just like off-the-rack clothing, you may find that you need a skirt size that is different from your sweater size. If you find yourself between sizes, you can experiment a bit with gauge. Knitting the second size at 4.75 stitches per inch rather than 5 stitches per inch will give you a hip size of 48.5 inches, for instance. The gauge on the skirt is considerably tighter than the gauge on the matching sweater. This makes the fabric of the skirt very firm and lessens the likelihood of unbecoming droopiness with wear. Knitting the mosaic border tightly is much more work than the body of the skirt, so don't despair.

A friend suggested you should alternate which side is the front every time you wear your knit skirt so it ages evenly. We'll let you decide for yourself if this is a good idea.

See Pattern Notes on pages 55–56 if you are new to mosaic knitting.

MOSAIC PATTERN

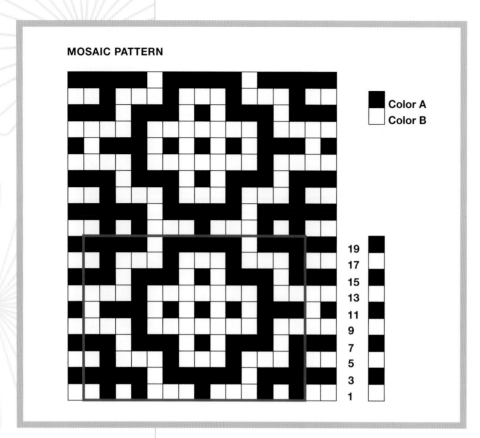

Color A
Color B

19
17
15
13
11
9
7
5
3
1

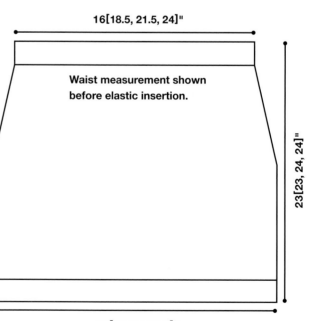

16[18.5, 21.5, 24]"

Waist measurement shown
before elastic insertion.

23[23, 24, 24]"

20[23, 26, 28.5]"

chapter 9

Accessories

Scarlett Carpetbag

Sunrise-Sunset Socks

Mimosa

Chinese Menu Handgear

Bluebelle Ruana

SIZE
One

FINISHED MEASUREMENTS
[in inches]
Length: 17
Height: 13
Gusset depth at bottom: 4.75

MATERIALS
S.R. Kertzer Butterfly Super-10
[100% cotton; 255 yds/230 m
per 125g skein]

[MC] 3995 Persian Red;
5 skeins

[CC] 3423 Red Coral; 2 skeins

1 24-inch US #5/3.75 mm
circular needle

Tapestry needle

1 yd fabric for lining

Sewing thread

Sewing needle or
sewing machine

Set of 4 bag feet

17-inch straight hex-open frame
*(See Shop Till You Drop,
page 157)*

Reinforcing material for main
panels and bottom of bag.
*Suggested materials are plastic
canvas (choose a very firm canvas) or cardboard covered with
adhesive shelf paper, or flexible
plastic sheets. Plastic canvas is
easy to sew into place, and a
piece of cardboard slid between
the fabric and the canvas adds
stability to the main panels.*

GAUGE
21 sts/21 rows = 4 inches in St
stitch after blocking

Scarlett Carpetbag

by Stephannie Roy

SOMEONE WE KNOW was once called "the Big Girl with the little purse" by a caring friend. He noticed that she was out of proportion with her tiny accessories…why didn't she? She gets it now. She'll be knitting Scarlett—a dramatic, functional bag that can hold a lot and still look hot. The bag is made of a substantial fabric and it's invisibly reinforced (with items you can find at a craft store) for added stability. We especially love the hardware: a super-cool hexagonal hinge that lets you open the bag really wide (and keep it open), and clever metal feet, to keep the bottom off the floor. The final touch is the linen-stitch strap: sturdy, nonstretchy, and very professional looking. People will ask where you got it!

Pattern

Yarn is used doubled throughout most of the pattern. Please read directions carefully.

MAIN PANELS (MAKE 2)

Hinge casing
Using a single strand of MC, CO 86 sts.
Beg with a RS row, work 7 rows in St st.
Next Row [WS]: K, to form turning edge for casing.

Panel
Add second strand of MC and work 6 rows in St st.
From this point, panel is worked with 2 strands of yarn.

Work all 30 rows of Chart A.
Work 6 rows of St st using MC.
Work all 30 rows of Chart B.
Work 6 rows of St st using MC.
BO all sts.

Gusset
Using 2 strands of MC, CO 6 sts.
Work 3 rows in Linen stitch.

Work m1 increases as follows: with left needle, lift strand between needles from back to front; purl lifted loop.
Increase Row [WS]: Sl1, m1, work in patt as set to last st, m1, p1.
Work 3 rows in patt as set, incorporating new sts into patt.
Repeat these 4 rows 5 times more. 18 sts.

Pattern Notes

LINEN STITCH (Worked over an even number of sts):
Row 1 [RS]: Sl1, [k1, sl1 with yarn in front] to last st, k1.
Row 2 [WS]: Sl1, [p1, sl1 with yarn in back] to last st, p1.
Repeat these 2 rows for Linen stitch.
When working Linen stitch, slip sts purlwise.

SLIP STITCH TIPS
If you've never done a slip stitch pattern before, do a larger-than-average swatch. It's important to get the hang of keeping the slipped strands loose or your fabric will pucker. So practice, practice, practice before you cast on for the bag.

LINING WORRIES
Is the idea of lining of this bag making you freak out? Pay a seamstress to do it for you!

Work *Increase Row.*
Work 5 rows in patt as set, incorporating new sts into patt.
Repeat these 6 rows 6 times more. 32 sts.

Cont in Linen stitch as set until work measures 31.5 inches, ending with a WS row.

Decrease Row [RS]: Sl1, ssk, work in patt as set to last 3 sts, k2tog, k1.
Work 5 rows in patt as set.
Repeat these 6 rows 6 times more. 18 sts rem.

Work *Decrease Row.* Work 3 rows in patt as set.
Repeat these 4 rows 5 times more. 6 sts rem.

BO rem sts.

HANDLES (MAKE 2)
Using 2 strands of MC, CO 6 sts.
Work in Linen stitch until work measures 24 inches, or desired length.
Straps will stretch slightly with use; if adding length, work straps slightly shorter than full desired length.

Finishing

Block all pieces.

LINING
The following instructions assume a 1-inch seam allowance.
Cut 2 rectangles of lining fabric that measure 24 by 14 inches. Lay them on a table, one on top of the other, right sides facing each other, with one long edge closest to you.
Pin them together at their lower corners, 1 inch in from side edges. Pin seams along the short edges that angle inwards towards the top of the bag, so that they are approx. 18.5 inches apart at the top edge. Trim seam allowances to 1 inch from pinned seam. Sew the two rectangles together along the seams you have marked.
Cut another rectangle that measures 7 inches by 15 inches. Pin this rectangle into the bottom (wider) end of the tube of lining you have prepared, so that the seams of the tube are at the centers of the short edges of the smaller rectangle. Sew together.

Assemble bag
Mark center point of Gusset, and of long edges (without hinge casing) of Main Panels.
Sew Gusset to Main Panels, beg at center point, working along bottom edge, then up side edges.
Cut 2 rectangles of reinforcing material, which measure 15.5 inches by 12.5 inches. Cut one rectangle which measures 4.25 inches by 12.5 inches. Stitch reinforcing materials in place; larger rectangles line Main Panels, smaller rectangle lines bottom of bag.
Attach bag feet as per instructions on package.
Sew lining into bag, so that top of lining ends at fold line of hinge casing.
Insert hinge and sew casing closed.
Sew handles securely to casing.

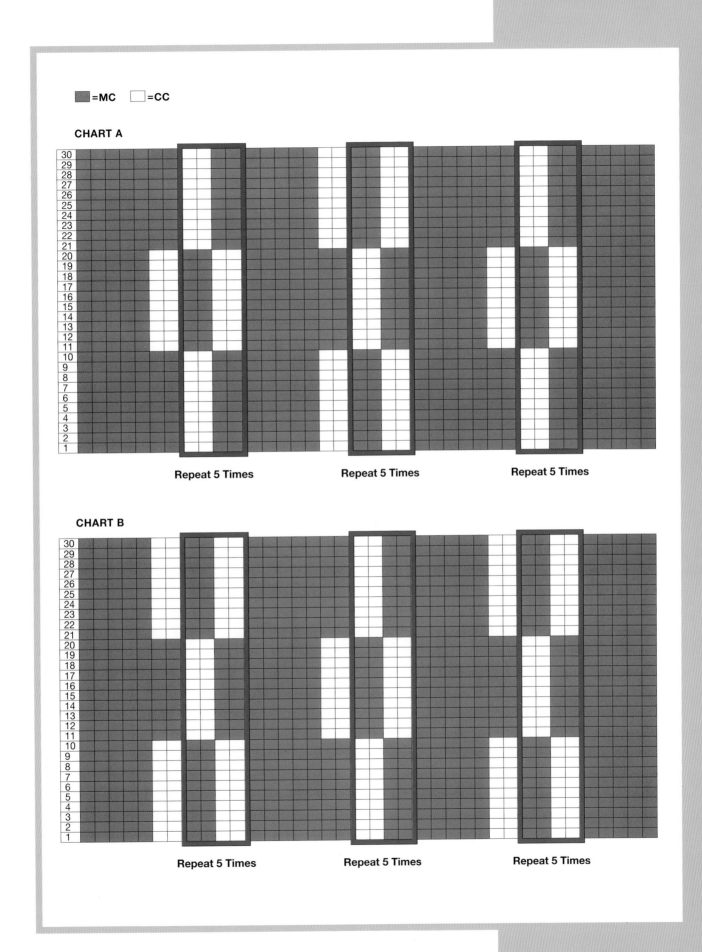

=MC ☐=CC

CHART A

Repeat 5 Times   Repeat 5 Times   Repeat 5 Times

CHART B

Repeat 5 Times   Repeat 5 Times   Repeat 5 Times

SIZE [in inches]
Foot length: 9.75
Foot circumference at instep: 10
Leg circumference above ankle bone: 9.75
Calf circumference (6–7 inches from base of heel): 15.75

FINISHED MEASUREMENTS [in inches]
Sock length: 9.75
Sock circumference at instep: 8.5
Sock circumference above ankle: 8.25
Sock circumference 6–7 inches from bottom of heel flap: 9.5 (unstretched)

MATERIALS
Lorna's Laces Shepherd Sock yarn [75% superwash wool, 25% nylon; 215 yds/197 m per 57g skein

[MC] Irving Park; 2 skeins

[CC] River; 1 skein

1 set [5] US #0/2 mm double-pointed needles

Safety pin or split ring marker

Stitch markers

Tapestry needle

GAUGE
36 sts/52 rnds =
4 inches in pattern st

Sunrise-Sunset Socks

by Jaya Srikrishnan

SOCKS? YES, SOCKS. Why? Because very few sock patterns take into consideration that your big bits don't stop at the knee. A lot of us have fat ankles. So what? We deserve handknit socks, too. This pattern is customizable to fit whatever you've got—wide feet, long feet, short feet, fat ankles, big calves. Knit 'em bright and show 'em off in a sweet pair of clogs. We think you have cute heels!

Pattern

CUFF
Using MC, CO 120 sts.
Divide sts evenly among 4 double-pointed needles and join to begin working in the round, being careful not to twist. Use safety pin or split ring marker to mark beg of round.

Round 1: [K2, p2] to end.
Work in 2 x 2 Rib as set for 29 rounds.

Next Round: Work Round 1 of Slip-Stitch pattern.
Next Round: Using CC, k4, work Round 2 of Slip-Stitch pattern.
Decrease Round: Using MC, k1, k2tog, k to last 3 sts, ssk, k1.
Cont working in Slip-Stitch pattern as set, working decreases as above on Rounds 3, 5 and 7 of pattern, and knitting first and last sts of all rounds (do not slip first st when working CC rounds) until 76 sts rem. Last decrease round will be Round 3 of Slip-Stitch pattern; cont working through rem rows of this repeat and 1 more repeat of

pattern with no further shaping, then work Round 1 once more.

HEEL FLAP
Work 19 sts of next row with CC in patt as set.
Turn work (so WS is facing); MC is at beg of round.
P19 with MC.
The 2 yarns, MC and CC, will be hanging opposite each other, with 38 sts between them and beg of round in the center. Transfer these sts to 1 needle; the heel flap will be worked back and forth on these 38 sts.
With WS facing, p all sts using CC; both yarns will now be at the same end of the heel flap, ready to work a RS row.
Row 1 [RS]: Using MC, [sl1, k1] to end.
Row 2 [WS]: Using MC, sl1, p to end.
Row 3 [RS]: Using CC, sl1, [sl1, k1] to last st, k1.
Row 4 [WS]: Using CC, sl1, p to end.
Repeat these 4 rows 8 times more, then work *Row 1 and Row 2* once more.

Pattern Notes

This pattern is designed to be easy to customize to fit your individual foot and leg. In general, unless there is a large difference in the circumference, the stitch count for the foot can be used for the ankle. If you use very different stitch counts, plan the pattern placement on the foot before you work the heel as the positioning of the heel might have to be adjusted slightly to result in a pleasing placement on the foot.

To ensure a sufficiently elastic CO edge, CO on over a larger needle, or two needles held together.

When working the Slip-Stitch pattern and heel flap, slipped sts are always slipped purlwise, with the yarn held to the back of the work. Work loosely, ensuring that the yarn is not pulled too tightly across the back of the work; it is important to maintain the elasticity of the fabric.

When working the leg of the sock, switch colors as follows:
• When switching from MC to CC, twist the colors together after the first st of the new round.
• When switching from CC to MC, twist the colors together after the last st of the previous round. **>>**

Twist colors by bringing the new color up underneath the strand of the old color, then dropping the old color. Maintain an even tension on the yarn at color changes, and give a gentle tug on the yarn being picked up to make sure that it is not too loose or too tight at the transition point. Make sure sts at the transition point are the same size and tension as the other sts.

When picking up gusset sts, you may wish to pick up an extra st between the gusset and the instep to prevent a hole. Work this extra st tog with the adjacent instep st on the next round.

When working the foot, do not twist yarns when changing colors; just pick up the new color and knit the next round. There will be a jog at the beginning of every 7th rnd. This is positioned on the sole so it is not noticeable. Pay attention to tension as you change yarns, make sure it remains consistent.

The ssk decrease is usually made by slipping two stitches knitwise to the right needle, then knitting them together through their back loops. For these socks, you might want to try slipping the second stitch purlwise instead of knitwise. The result is a mirror image of the k2tog decrease, and will result in more symmetrical decreases.

SLIP-STITCH PATTERN
(Worked over a multiple of 4 sts):
Rounds 1, 3, 5, 7: K all sts using MC.
Rounds 2, 4, 6: [Sl1, k3] to end using CC.
Repeat these 7 rounds for Slip-Stitch pattern.

Turn heel
Heel is turned using MC only.
Row 1: Sl1, k24, ssk, turn work.
Row 2: Sl1, p12, p2tog, turn work.
Row 3: Sl1, k12, ssk, turn work.
Row 4: Sl1, p12, p2tog, turn work.
Repeat *Rows 3 and 4* until all sts have been worked; 14 sts on needle.

GUSSET
Next Round: Using CC, k all 14 heel sts, pick up and k 19 sts along edge of heel flap, place marker, work all 38 held sts from top of foot in patt as set (round 2 of patt), place marker, pick up and k 19 sts along rem edge of heel flap.
(XX) This point will be the new beg of round; mark with safety pin or split ring marker. 90 sts.
While working the gusset, the Slip-Stitch pattern will only be worked on the 38 sts between markers at the top of the foot. The color used for each round will not be specified in the following directions; use the color needed for next round of Slip-Stitch pattern.

Next Round: K to 3 sts before marker, ssk, k1, work sts between markers in Slip-Stitch pattern, k1, k2tog, k to end of round.
Next Round: K to marker, work next round of Slip-Stitch pattern to next marker, k to end.
Repeat these 2 rounds 4 times more; 80 sts rem.

Redistribute sts as follows: place st before first marker and first 19 of sts between markers on one needle, place rem 19 of sts between markers and st after second marker on second needle, divide rem sts between 2 needles; 20 sts on each needle. The 40 sts on the top of the foot will be worked in Slip-Stitch pattern, rem 40 sts will be worked in St st. Remove first and second markers on next round; retain end-of-round marker.

Work in patt until work measures 8.25 inches from back of heel.

TOE (YY)
Break CC; toe will be worked using MC only. Remove rem marker, k to end of needle; yarn should now be at center bottom of foot. Designate the next needle N1, the foll 2 needles (top of foot) N2 and N3, and the last needle N4.

Decrease Round: K to last 3 sts on N1, ssk, k1; k1, k2tog, k to end of N2; k to last 3 sts of N3, ssk, k1; k1, k2tog, k to end of N4.
Next Round: K all sts.
Repeat these 2 rounds 7 times more. 48 sts rem.

Work *Decrease Round* only 4 times more. 32 sts rem.
K to end of N1.
Place all sts from N1 and N4 on N1, place all sts from N2 and N3 on N2.
Graft sts from N1 to sts from N2.

Finishing

Weave in ends.

Making Socks Fit Your Feet (and Calves)

Let's take a look at the various parts of a sock and see how some measurements and a few calculations will help create a perfect-fitting sock.

Stuff you'll need:
- paper and pencil
- measuring tape
- 12- to 18-inch ruler
- calculator
- stitch (**S**) and row (**R**) gauges

Now it's time for some measuring. Like the other number-driven parts of this book, we'll go through an exercise first with one of our Big Girl's feet so you get the concepts. Your chart is at the end.

Code	What am I measuring/ calculating?	Our Big Girl's numbers
S	Stitch gauge **per inch**	9
R	Row gauge **per inch**	13
A	circumference of the widest part of your foot	9.5"
B	circumference of your ankle just above the ankle bone	10"
C	length of your foot (use a ruler)	9.75"
D	circumference of your leg where sock ends	12"
E	height of point **D** from the floor (use a ruler)	7.5"

The first step is to figure out the **S** (stitch gauge) your yarn, needles and stitch pattern will give. For this exercise, our Big Girl is using the gauge in the sock pattern on page 136:

36 stitches/52 rounds = 4 inches *or*
9 stitches/13 rounds = 1 inch

We really only need to deal with our Big Girl's **S** number right now–it's 9. Her **R** number is 13. We won't need **R** for a while.

LEG

How many stitches should I cast on?

Multiply the circumference of your leg (**D**) by the stitch gauge (**S**). Then you need to decide how you like your socks to fit. The recommended fit is slightly snug, because socks usually stretch a little as you wear them. For the recommended snug fit, subtract 15% or multiply by 0.85. If you prefer an even snugger fit, subtract 20% or multiply by 0.8. People with circulation problems, or Big Girls whose feet and ankles swell during the day should use a looser fit. Simply subtract 10% or multiply by 0.9. For all fit variations, remember to round up or down to the nearest multiple of 4.

The same fit multiplier does not have to be used for all calculations. For example, if your ankles swell but your feet never do, you might subtract 10% at the ankle but 20% at the foot.

Our Big Girl likes her socks a little snug, so she'll use the recommended snug fit numbers. They look like this:

$$D \times S \times 0.85 = F \text{ (number of stitches to cast on)}$$
12 inches x 9 stitches per inch x 0.85 =
91.8 stitches

Our Big Girl rounds this to the nearest multiple of 4, so she will cast on 92 stitches to start her sock at the leg.

How many stitches do I want at the ankle?

This is just like working the cast-on count. You multiply the circumference of your ankle (**B**) by your stitch gauge (**S**) to get your stitch count at the ankle (**G**). Our Big Girl plugs in her numbers.

$$B \times S \times 0.85 = G$$
10 inches x 9 stitches per inch x 0.85 =
76.5 stitches, rounded to 76.

If **F** and **G** are within 4 to 8 stitches of each other, use the same number for both. If the numbers are farther apart, use the actual numbers. Our Big Girl has 16 stitches between **F** and **G**, so she'll use the actual numbers.

How many stitches at the foot?

You know the drill. The new variable here is **H** (number of stitches at the foot). Don't forget the rounding up or down to the nearest multiple of 4.

$$A \times S \times 0.85 = H$$
9.5 inches x 9 stitches per inch x 0.85 =
72.675 stitches, rounded to 72.

Flap This!

A few things in sock knitting are standardized, which we like. Here's the first one: No matter the size of your foot, allot **3.5** inches for the heel flap. That's easy.

Now you can figure out how to shape the calf.

First you figure out how many inches of height are in the leg (**I**) after you subtract the height of the heel—remember we said it's always 3.5 inches.

$$E - 3.5 = I$$
7.5 inches – **3.5** inches = 4 inches

So our Big Girl has 4 inches of sock leg to knit. That number is easily converted to rounds (**J**) with a little math.

$$I \times R = J$$
4 inches x 13 rounds per inch = 52 rounds

Right. 4 inches is the same as 52 rounds. Now you figure out how many stitches you need to decrease (**K**) between the top of the sock (**F**) and the ankle (**G**).

$$F - G = K$$
92 stitches – 76 stitches = 16 stitches

16 stitches need to be decreased between the top of the sock and the ankle. Don't forget to divide **K** by 2, because decreases are always done in pairs. That's how you get **L**.

$$K \div 2 = L$$
16 decreases ÷ 2 = 8 pairs of decreases

Now you just divide the number of rounds (**J**) by the number of pairs of decreases (**L**), and voila. Decrease rate **M**! If you get a fraction, round **M** up or down to the nearest whole number.

$$J \div L = M$$
52 rounds ÷ 8 decreases = 6.5

She rounds to the nearest whole number, so she'll decrease every 7 rounds for her leg shaping.

What's left? The foot!

Easy peasy lemon squeezy! The length of your foot (**C**) minus room for your toes (another handy constant – allow **1.75** inches for the toe-shaped area) gives you the length of your sock's foot without shaping (**C1**).

$$C - 1.75 = C1$$
9.75 inches – 1.75 inches = 8 inches

HEEL FLAP

The height of the heel flap is constant – 3.5 inches for all of us. But the width (**N**)? That varies based on the width of our foot. Thankfully, the heel flap is generally worked on half the number of stitches we're working at the ankle (**G**). That makes it easy to figure out.

$$G \div 2 = N$$
76 stitches ÷ 2 = 38 stitches

So our Big Girl's heel flap is 38 stitches wide.

The number of rows in the flap (**O**) is equal to the number of stitches in the flap. This is another one of those standardized sock knitting rules. Just go with it.

$$N = O$$
38 = 38

Handy heel flap stitch trick: The first stitch of each row is slipped purlwise to make it easy to pick up stitches for the gusset. This gives you a rectangular flap because the stitch patterns used on the heel tend to pull in width-wise. Looks nice.

Turn that heel!

The sock pattern on page 136 uses a square heel. How do you do that? Like this!

Mark the center of the heel flap with a stitch marker. Take your **N** number (38, for our Big Girl) and divide by **2**. So in this case, the marker would be between the 19th and 20th stitches.

The width of the heel is **14** stitches (12 center stitches and 1 stitch on each side which represents the decrease at each end). Why **14**? It's another standardized sock number.

Don't forget the heel flap stitch trick – slip the first stitch of every row purlwise.

Row 1: Slip 1, knit to 6 stitches past the center marker (in our case, 24 stitches: 19 + 6 = 25. Then subtract 1 for the slipped stitch). Then slip-slip-knit (ssk) and turn leaving the remaining stitches unworked.

Row 2: Slip 1, work the 12 center stitches, then purl 2 together and turn.

From now on, each RS row will be worked like this: sl 1, k 12, ssk, turn. Each WS row will be worked like this: sl 1, p 12, p2tog, turn.

Repeat these rows until all the stitches have been worked.

Picking up and knitting the gusset

Once the heel turn is completed, pick up 1 stitch for each 2 rows in the heel flap. *Since the first stitch of each row was slipped, picking up 1 stitch in each of those slipped stitches means you pick up the right number of stitches every time. We told you it was a handy trick!*

Turn the work and knit across all the heel stitches (14 in our example), using the instructions in the pattern for which color yarn to use. Pick up 19 stitches (1 for each 2 rows of the 38 row heel flap) across one side of the flap. Knit across the instep stitches in the established pattern, following instructions in the sock pattern. Pick up 19 stitches on the other side of the heel flap. From now on the knitting will be in the round. Follow the sock pattern instructions from point **XX** on page 138 to work the 2 rounds of the gusset (one decrease round and one plain round) until only the number of stitches at **G** remain (for our Big Girl, that'd be 76).

TOE

To work the toe, follow the instructions in the sock pattern from point **YY** on page 138. Half the number of stitches to be decreased are decreased every other round. The remaining number are decreased every round.

In the example, the foot has 72 stitches (**H**). According to the pattern, 32 stitches are left at the end of the toe shaping. So 72 − 32 = 40 stitches need to be decreased in the toe shaping. Of these, 20 stitches will be decreased at an every-other-round rate and 20 at an every-round rate. Follow Rounds 1 and 2 of the toe shaping in the sock pattern till 52 stitches remain. Then work Round 2 only till 32 stitches remain.

You know how to finish…just weave in your ends!

Here's your own handy custom sock chart. Photocopy it and fill it in when you start a new pair of socks. And at least once a year, remeasure your feet. Why? Because foot size and shape can change with age, pregnancy, or weight. If you're going to the trouble of making socks that really fit, make sure they really will!

Code	What am I measuring/calculating?	My numbers
S	Stitch gauge **per inch**	
R	Row gauge **per inch**	
A	circumference of the widest part of your foot	
B	circumference of your ankle just above the ankle bone:	
C	length of your foot (use a ruler)	
C1	length of the foot of your sock without toe shaping (**C − 1.75**)	
D	circumference of your leg where sock ends	
E	height of point **D** from the floor (use a ruler)	
F	number of stitches to cast on *round up or down to the nearest multiple of 4:* for recommended snug fit: (**D x S**) x 0.85 for looser fit: (**D x S**) x 0.9 for super-snug fit: (**D x S**) x 0.8	
G	stitch count at ankle: (**B x S**) x fit multiplier *round up or down to the nearest multiple of 4*	
H	stitch count for foot: (**A x S**) x fit multiplier	
I	length of leg available for shaping = **E − 3.5"**	
J	number of rounds available for shaping = **I x R**	
K	total number of stitches to be decreased = **F − G**	
L	number of decrease rounds needed = **K ÷ 2**	
M	decrease rate; this is read as 'decrease every **M** rounds' = **J ÷ L**	
N	number of sts for the heel flap = **G ÷ 2**	
O	number of rows in the heel flap = same as **N**	
P	number of gusset stitches to pick up on each side of the heel flap = **N ÷ 2**	

FINISHED MEASUREMENTS
[in inches]
90 from tip to tip
35 long at center back

MATERIALS
Euroflax Linen Sport Weight
distributed by Louet Sales
[100% linen; 270 yds/243 m per
100g skein]; color: Crabapple
Blossom; 6 skeins

1 47-inch US #5/3.75mm
circular needle

1 24-inch US #5/3.75mm
circular needle

1,645 size 6/0 silverlined
crystal seed beads

Dental floss threader or
big-eyed bead needle

Safety pin or split ring marker

2 stitch markers

Tapestry needle

GAUGE
19 sts/28 rows = 4 inches in St
stitch, after washing, machine
drying, and blocking

Mimosa

by Sivia Harding

IF YOU LOVE WRAPS, knit yourself this big, beautiful, beaded baby that shimmers and catches the light. A variation on the usual triangle creates a wider and shallower wrap, so it covers you generously without cupping your butt. Additional shaping at the shoulder and back neck give a great Big Girl fit. Two methods of placing beads are used, one while working from the right side and one while working from the wrong side, cleverly enabling lace, shaping, and beads to mesh together seamlessly. Shall we dance?

Pattern

CAST ON AND LOWER EDGING

Thread 491 (or more) beads onto yarn. Push the beads several meters down the yarn; they will not be used in the first few rows.
Leaving a tail of several inches and using an overhand knot, knot together the end of the beaded yarn with the end of another ball of yarn. (This knot will be undone later, and the tails woven in.) CO 599 sts using the long-tail cast on method. After casting on, cut second strand of yarn, leaving a generous tail to weave in later.

K 2 rows.
Next Row [RS]: [K3, SF] to last 3 sts, k3. 149 beads placed.
K 2 rows.
Next Row [WS]: K3, p to last 3 sts, k3.

BEADED MIMOSA BORDER

Set-up Row [RS]: Sl 1, k1, ssk, k49, place marker, work Row 1 of Border Chart 19 times, place marker, k48, k2tog, k2. 597 sts.
Next Row [WS]: Sl 1, k2, p to last 3 sts, k3. (This counts as Row 2 of Border Chart.)

Next Row [RS]: Sl 1, k1, ssk, k to marker, work next row of Border Chart 19 times, k to last 4 sts, k2tog, k2.
Next Row [WS]: Sl 1, k2, p to marker, work next row of Border Chart 19 times, p to last 3 sts, k3.
Repeat these 2 rows 8 times more, working through all rows of Border Chart. 541 sts rem.

BODY PATTERN

Set-up Row 1 [RS]: Sl1, k1, sl1-k2tog-psso, k to marker, [k8, sl1-k2tog-psso, YO, k1, YO, k3tog, k9] 9 times, k8, sl1-k2tog-psso, YO, k1; place safety pin or split ring marker in st just worked, as

Pattern Notes

SB: *Slip bead into place while working a WS row:* Bring yarn to back (RS) of work, slip next st purlwise, slide a bead up the yarn until it is as close as possible to the right hand needle, bring yarn to front of work, ready to purl the next st, leaving bead positioned in back of slipped st, on RS of work.

SF: *Slip bead into place while working a RS row:* Bring yarn to front (RS) of work, slip next st purlwise, slide a bead up the yarn until it is as close as possible to the right hand needle, bring yarn to back of work, ready to knit the next st, leaving the bead positioned in front of the slipped st, on RS of work.

BEADED LACE STEM PATTERN (Worked over a multiple of 22 sts):
Row 1 [RS]: K8, ssk, YO, k1, YO, k2tog, k9.
Row 2 [WS]: P all sts.
Row 3 [RS]: K8, ssk, YO, k1, YO, k2tog, k9.
Row 4 [WS]: P8, SB, p5, SB, p7 »

THREADING BEADS ONTO YARN WITH A DENTAL FLOSS THREADER: A dental floss threader is what people use to thread floss around their dental braces and bridges. It is semi-rigid plastic and is made up of a loop and a "joined" section. Thread the knitting yarn through the loop and pick up beads with the working end of the needle. Then slide the beads over the loop and onto the knitting yarn.

String only enough beads for the skein of yarn you are working on. Do not try to string all 1,645 beads at once! Here is the breakdown of beads used per skein of yarn for the sample shawl: skein 1, 491 beads; skein 2, 304 beads; skein 3, 246 beads; skein 4, 292 beads; skein 5, 312 beads. Your breakdown may be different due to variations in knitting style, so string on a few more beads than you think you will need.

When working the shawl, it will be necessary to stop frequently to push to beads futher down the working yarn. Read ahead to see if you will need to incorporate beads into the row you are about to knit; if not, take a moment to push the beads several meters further along the yarn.

The first st of each row is slipped purlwise. Work the first and last 3 sts of each row loosely to avoid binding at the edge.

An ssk decrease is usually made by slipping two stitches knitwise to the right needle, then knitting them together through their back loops. For this shawl, you might want to try slipping the second stitch purlwise instead of knitwise. The result is a mirror image of the k2tog decrease, and will give nicer symmetry to the lace patterns.

---

this will be the center st; YO, k3tog, k9, [k8, sl1-k2tog-psso, YO, k1, YO, k3tog, k9] 9 times, k to last 5 sts, k3tog, k2. 499 sts rem.

Set-up Row 2 [WS]: Sl 1, k2, p to last 3 sts, k3.

Set-up Row 3 [RS]: Sl 1, k1, ssk, k to marker, work Row 3 of Beaded Lace Stem pattern 9 times, k7, sl1-k2tog-psso, YO, k1, YO, k3tog, k8, work Row 3 of Beaded Lace Stem pattern 9 times, k to last 4 sts, k2tog, k2. 495 sts rem.

Set-up Row 4 [WS]: Sl 1, k2, p to marker, work Row 4 of Beaded Lace Stem pattern 9 times, p7, SB, p5, SB, p6, work Row 4 of Beaded Lace Stem pattern 9 times, p to last 3 sts, k3.

Pattern Row 1 [RS]: Sl 1, sl1-k2tog-psso, work in patt as set (Row 1 of Beaded Lace Stem pattern) to 3 sts before center st, sl1-k2tog-psso, YO, k1, YO, k3tog, work in patt as set to last 5 sts, k3tog, k2.

Pattern Row 2 [WS]: Sl 1, k2, p to last 3 sts, k3.

Pattern Row 3 [RS]: Sl 1, ssk, work in patt as set (Row 3 of Beaded Lace Stem pattern) to 3 sts before center st, sl1-k2tog-psso, YO, k1, YO, k3tog, work in patt as set to last 4 sts, k2tog, k2.

Pattern Row 4 [RS]: Sl 1, k2, work in patt as set (Row 4 of Beaded Lace Stem pattern) to 3 sts before center st, SB, p5, SB, work in patt as set to last 3 sts, k3.

Repeat Pattern Rows 1–4 39 times more, then work *Pattern Row 1* again. 89 sts rem.

Maintaining pattern while decreasing

As the shawl is shaped by the decreases at the outer edges and center, the number of repeats of the Beaded Lace Stem pattern will decrease. Remove the markers that delineate the areas of St st at the sides of the shawl, once these areas have been decreased away.

On *Pattern Row 4,* do not place beads within 3 sts of the 3-st garter st border at the beginning and end of the row. Do not place beads within 2 sts of the central beaded lace column.

On *Pattern Rows 1* and *3,* do not work the [ssk, YO, k1, YO, k2tog] sequence unless there are at least 3 sts between this sequence and the shaping decreases. Work these sts in St st instead.

Every few rows, move the marker in the center st up to a row closer to the needle; do not lose sight of the center st.

Switch to shorter needle when desired.

NECKBAND EDGING

Next Row [WS]: Sl 1, k to end.
Next Row [RS]: Sl 1, k1, ssk, k39, sl1-k2tog-psso, k39, k2tog, k2. 85 sts rem.
Next Row [WS]: Sl 1, k to end.
Next Row [RS]: Sl 1, k1, ssk, [SF, k3] 9 times, SF, sl1-k2tog-psso, [SF, k3] 9 times, SF, k2tog, k2. 81 sts rem.
Next Row [WS]: Sl 1, k to end.
Next Row [RS]: Sl 1, k1, ssk, k35, sl1-k2tog-psso, k35, k2tog, k2. 77 sts rem.
BO all sts loosely.

Finishing

Undo knot from CO and weave in ends. Weave in all rem ends.
When weaving in ends, bulk can be reduced by splitting the strand into several plies and weaving each in separately, in different directions. This takes more time, but with a smooth fabric like this, you will notice the difference!

Linen is best finished by washing and drying in a machine, which makes the fiber both softer and stronger. However, because of the beads, I would not recommend washing this shawl in a washing machine. Instead, soak the finished shawl in very hot water for ½ hour, squeeze, place in a zippered mesh bag, and dry it in a dryer. The shawl will emerge soft and dry, and wadded into a ball. Don't worry! Spread it out on a bed or carpet and mist the surface lightly with water. Pat out, stretching where necessary, to correspond with given measurements.

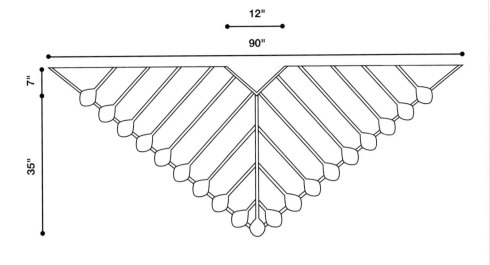

12"

90"

7"

35"

BORDER CHART

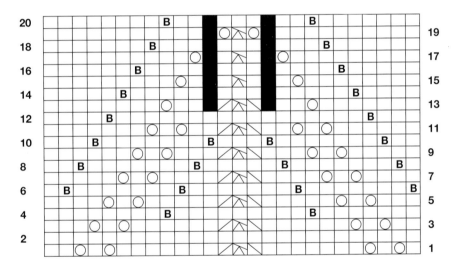

20								19
18								17
16								15
14								13
12								11
10								9
8								7
6								5
4								3
2								1

☐   K on RS, P on WS

◹   K2tog

◺   Ssk

⧄   Sl 1-k2tog-psso

◯   YO

▮   No stitch

B   SB – Slip bead into place while working a WS row; Bring yarn to back (RS) of work, slip next st purlwise, slide a bead up the yarn until it is as close as possible to the right needle, bring yarn to front of work, ready to purl the next st, leaving bead positioned in back of slipped st, on RS of work.

SIZE
M[L, 1X, 2X, 3X]

FINISHED MEASUREMENTS
[in inches]
Wrist circumference: varies
with cuff option; approx. 1 inch
less than hand circumference
Hand circumference: 6.5[7.5,
8.5, 9.5, 10.5]

MATERIALS
Jo Sharp Silkroad DK [80%
wool, 10% silk, 5% cashmere;
147 yds/135 m per 50g skein];
color: 419 Butternut (mittens)/
412 Beanshoot (gloves);
2 balls per pair

2 24-inch US #5/3.75mm
circular needles

1 set US #5/3.75mm straight or
double-point needles (for Ruffled
Cuff only)

1 24-inch US #3/3.25mm
circular needle or set of straight
needles (for Garter Cuff only)

Stitch marker

Stitch holders or waste yarn

Tapestry needle

GAUGE
24 sts/32 rows =
4 inches in St stitch

Chinese Menu Handgear

by Carol J. Sulcoski

IF YOU LOOK AT WOMEN'S HANDS, you'll soon notice that there is really no relationship between body size and hand size. There are Big Girls with relatively small hands, petite girls with super-long fingers, and every combination in between. So, here's a customizable pattern that lets you pick one element from Column A, one from Column B. The result: truly individualized, truly comfortable handgear. Pick gloves or mittens, long cuffs or short, with hand and finger length tailored to your very own match. Now that's handy! And no one said you have to make just one pair.

Pattern

CUFF

Option 1: Ruffled cuff

Using straight or double-point needles, CO 36[42, 48, 54, 60] sts.
Beg with WS row, work 7 rows in St st.
Next Row [RS]: [K6, twist] to last 6 sts, k6.
P 1 row using larger circular needle.
Divide sts between larger circular needles and join to begin working in the round, being careful not to twist.
Work in St st until work measures 1.5 inches, or desired length.

Next Round: [K12[14, 16, 18, 10], m1] 3 times. 39[45, 51, 57, 63] sts.
Proceed to HAND.

Option 2: Picot hem

Using larger circular needle, CO 33[39, 45, 51, 57] sts. Divide evenly between larger circular needles, placing 1 more st on the first needle than on the second needle. Join to begin working in the round, being careful not to twist.
K 4 rounds.

Next Round: K1, [YO, k2tog] to end of round. (This round forms the turning round.)
K 7 rounds.
P 2 rounds.
Cont in St st for 0.5 inch further, or to desired cuff length from turning round.

Next Round: [K5[6, 7, 8, 9], m1] 6 times, k3. 39[45, 51, 57, 63] sts.
Proceed to HAND.

Option 3: Twisted rib

Using larger circular needle, CO 36[40, 48, 52, 60] sts. Divide evenly between larger circular needles and join to begin working in the round, being careful not to twist.

Pattern Notes

Pattern is worked in the round on two circular needles.
- Choose your size based on your hand circumference, measured between web of thumb and knuckles.
- Select a cuff, and work to desired length.
- Continue by working directions for hand, which are the same for all styles.
- Proceed to the directions for MITTEN or GLOVE, as preferred.
- Finally, work the thumb.
- Try on the mitten or each finger of the glove before starting decreases, to ensure the finished item is the perfect length for your hand or fingers.

TWIST (FOR RUFFLED CUFF): With the point between the last st worked and the next st as a pivot point, rotate your left needle 360 degrees. The CO edge and the rows you have knit will twist up between the needles and curl down beneath your needle again, so you are ready to keep knitting. When subsequent rows have been knit, this twisted edge forms wavy scallops.

Rounds 1, 2, and 4: [P2, k2] to end.
Round 3: [P2, k2tog but do not drop sts from left needle, k into first of these sts again, drop both sts from left needle] to end.
Repeat these 4 rounds until work measures 2.5 inches or desired length, ending with *Round 4.*

K 1 round.
Next Round: [K12[8, 16, 10, 20], m1] 3[5, 3, 5, 3] times, k0[0, 0, 2, 0]. spruce 39[45, 51, 57, 63] sts.
Proceed to HAND.

Option 4: Garter cuff
Using smaller circular needle, CO 32[38, 44, 50, 56] sts.
Work in garter stitch (k every row) until work measures 2.5 inches, or desired length.

Next Row [RS]: Using larger needles, [k4[5, 6, 7, 8], m1] 7 times, k4[3, 2, 1, 0]. 39[45, 51, 57, 63] sts.
Divide evenly between larger circular needles and join to begin working in the round, being careful not to twist.
K 1 round.
Proceed to HAND.

HAND
All sizes are worked on an odd number of sts. Distribute sts so first needle of round has 1 st more than second needle. On rounds where directions differ for sts on first and second needles, the row will be divided by a semi-colon. You may want to place a safety pin in your work to mark beg of round.

Next Round: K to last st of first needle, place marker, k last st on first needle; k to end of round. Sts between marker and end of first neeedle will be referred to as gusset sts.

Shape thumb gusset
Next Round: K to marker, slip marker, m1, k rem sts on first needle, m1; k all sts on second needle.
K 2 rounds.

Repeat these 3 rounds 5[6, 7, 8, 8] times more. 13[15, 17, 19, 19] sts in gusset.

Try on mitten and ensure that gusset is deep enough: work should reach top of web between thumb and hand. If gusset is not deep enough, work extra gusset rounds without shaping as necessary.

Next Round: Work to marker, place gusset sts on waste yarn or st holder, CO 2 sts in space left by gusset sts; k all sts on second needle.
K 1 round. 40[46, 52, 58, 64] sts.
Place last st of first needle on second needle; each needle has 20[23, 26, 29, 32] sts.
Proceed to MITTEN or GLOVE.

MITTEN
Work in St st until work measures 1[1.5, 1.5, 2, 2] inches less than desired finished length.

Next Round: [K1, ssk, k to last 3 sts on needle, k2tog, k1] on each needle.
Next Round: K all sts.
Repeat these 2 rounds 4[5, 6, 7, 8] times more. 20[22, 24, 26, 28] sts rem.

Next Round: [K2tog] to end of round.
Break yarn, draw tail through rem sts and pull tight. Proceed to THUMB.

GLOVE
Work in St st until work reaches base of fingers.
For extra width in fingers, CO 3 sts instead of 2 in gaps between fingers. This will give you 1 extra stitch for Little and Index fingers, and 2 extra sts for Ring and Middle fingers.

Little finger
Next Round: K4[4, 5, 5, 6], place rem sts from first needle on waste yarn or st holder, CO 2 sts, place first 16[18, 21, 23, 26] sts of second needle on waste yarn or st holder, k rem 4[4, 5, 5, 6] sts from second needle.
Work these 10[10, 12, 12, 14] sts in St st to desired length.

Next Round: [K2tog] to end of round. Break yarn, draw tail through rem sts and pull tight.

Ring finger

Using first needle, k first 5[6, 6, 7, 7] sts of held sts from first needle (adjacent to Little finger), CO 2 sts; using second needle, k last 5[6, 6, 7, 7] sts of held sts from second needle, pick up and k 1 st in each of the 2 CO sts from previous finger. 14[16, 16, 18, 18] sts. Work in St st to desired length.

Next Round: [K2tog] to end of round. Break yarn, draw tail through rem sts and pull tight.

Middle finger

Using first needle, k first 5[6, 7, 8, 9] sts of held sts from first needle (adjacent to Little finger), CO 2 sts; using second needle, k last 5[6, 7, 8, 9] sts of held sts from second needle, pick up and k 1 st in each of the 2 CO sts from previous finger. 14[16, 18, 20, 22] sts. Work in St st to desired length.

Next Round: [K2tog] to end of round. Break yarn, draw tail through rem sts and pull tight.

Index finger

Using first needle, k rem 6[7, 8, 9, 10] held sts from first needle; using second needle, k rem 6[7, 8, 9, 10] held sts from second needle, pick up and k 1 st in each of the 2 CO sts from previous finger. 14[16, 18, 20, 22] sts. Work in St st to desired length.

Next Round: [K2tog] to end of round. Break yarn, draw tail through rem sts and pull tight.

Thumb

Remove thumb sts fron st holder or waste yarn and divide between first and second needle. Pick up and k 1 st in each CO st. Work in St st to desired length.

Next Round: [K2tog] to end of round. Break yarn, draw tail through rem sts and pull tight.

Finishing

For Ruffled Cuff and Garter Cuff, sew ends of cuff together.
For Picot Hem Cuff, fold hem to inside along turning round, and sew in place. (Do not sew a tight seam that will prevent cuff from stretching!)
Weave in ends.

SIZE
One

FINISHED MEASUREMENTS
[in inches]
Width: 46
Length: 30 (not including hood)

MATERIALS
Lorna's Laces Fisherman
[100% wool; 500 yds/457 m per
8oz skein]

[MC] Violet; 5 skeins

[CC] Tahoe; 1 skein

1 set US #8/5mm
double-pointed needles

1 36-inch US #8/5mm
circular needle

1 spare 24-inch [or longer]
US #8/5mm [or smaller] circular
needle will be used to hold
stitches.

1 large stitch holder

Safety pins

Tapestry needle

CD case

GAUGE
20 sts/26 rows =
4 inches in St stitch

Bluebelle Ruana

by Kate Gilbert

PONCHO? Please don't. You might as well wrap yourself in the blanket from your bed. Instead, choose a ruana. This elegantly draped, hooded beauty will skim your body, not overwhelm you with bulky knitted fabric. And unlike most wraps, this one is cleverly constructed to stay on. It's the Big Girl alternative to a coat, perfect for cool days when a coat would be too warm. Wear it wrapped around your shoulders, or just draped. Please do!

Pattern

RIGHT FRONT
Using Crochet Cast On, and CC, CO 4 sts.
Work CC, work 81 rows of i-cord (measures approx. 12.5 inches).

Place sts on safety pin.
Using circular needle, and MC, pick up and K 65 sts along length of i-cord just worked (approx. 4 sts for every 5 rows).
Odd-numbered Rows 1–45 [WS]: P.
Row 2: K to end, CO 8 sts. 73 sts.
Row 4: K to end, CO 5 sts. 78 sts.
Row 6: K to end, CO 4 sts. 82 sts.
Rows 8 and 10: K to end, CO 3 sts. 88 sts.
Rows 12–22: K to end, CO 2 sts. 100 sts.
Rows 24–42: K to last st, m1, k1. 110 sts.
Row 44: K.
Row 46: K to last st, m1, k1.
Repeat *Rows 43–46* 4 times more. 115 sts.

Cont in St st until work measures 32 inches or desired length to shoulder, ending with a RS row.

Place all sts on st holder, scrap yarn, or spare needle. Do not break yarn.

RIGHT BACK
Using Crochet Cast On and CC, CO 4 sts.
Work 81 rows of i-cord, (measures approx. 12.5 inches) place sts on safety pin.

Using circular needle, and MC, pick up and K 65 sts along length of i-cord just worked (approx. 4 sts for every 5 rows).
Row 1 [WS]: P.
Even-numbered Rows 2–22: K.
Row 3 [WS]: P to end, CO 8 sts. 73 sts.
Row 5 [WS]: P to end, CO 5 sts. 78 sts.
Row 7 [WS]: P to end, CO 4 sts. 82 sts.
Rows 9 and 11 [WS]: P to end, CO 3 sts. 88 sts.
Odd-numbered Rows 13–23 [WS]: P to end, CO 2 sts. 100 sts.
Even-numbered Rows 24–42 [RS]: K1, m1, k to end. 110 sts.
Odd-numbered Rows 25–45 [WS]: P.

Pattern Notes

I-CORD: Using a double-pointed needle, CO 4 sts. K all sts.
Next Row: Instead of turning the work around to work back on the WS, slide all sts to the other end of the needle, switch the needle back to your left hand, bring the yarn around the back of the work, and start knitting the sts again.
Repeat this row to form i-cord. After a few rows, the work will begin to form a tube.

APPLIED I-CORD: With RS of work facing and using cable or twisted loop method, CO 4 sts. (Cast these new sts on in addition to picked-up sts already on needle.)
Next Row: Using a double-pointed needle, k3, ssk. (Last i-cord st has been worked together with first picked-up st on needle.) Slide 4 sts just worked to other end of a double-pointed needle and bring yarn around back of work, ready to begin working the next row.
Repeat this row until all picked-up sts have been worked. BO rem sts.

Row 44: K.
Row 46: K1, m1, k to end.
Repeat *Rows 43–46* 4 times more.
115 sts.

Cont in St st until work measures 32 inches or desired length to shoulder, ending with a RS row. Break yarn; leave sts on needle.

Starting at outside (curved) edge, using Three-Needle Bind Off, a double-point needle, and ball of yarn attached to Right Front, join first 93 sts of Right Front and Right Back. 22 sts rem on each Front and Back, 1 st rem on working needle. P st from working needle and all Right Front sts onto needle holding Right Back. 45 sts.

RIGHT HOOD
Work 6 rws in St st, ending with a WS row.
Next Row: K to last st, m1, k1.
Work 11 rows in St st.
Repeat these 12 rows 5 times more.
51 sts. Hood measures 12 inches.

Row 1: K.
Row 2: P43, W&T.
Row 3: K to end.
Row 4: P35,, W&T.
Row 5: K to end.
Row 6: P27, W&T.
Row 7: K to end.
Row 8: P19, W&T.
Row 9: K to end.
Row 10: P11, W&T.
Row 11: K to end.
Row 12: P all sts. When you encounter a wrapped st, pick up the wrap and place it on the left needle, then p it tog with the wrapped st.

LEFT BACK
Work as for Right Front.

LEFT FRONT
Work as for Right Back.
Starting at outside (curved) edge, using Three-Needle Bind Off, a double-point

needle, and the ball of yarn attached to Left Back, join first 93 sts of Left Front and Left Back. 22 sts rem on Front and Back each, 1 st rem on working needle. P st from working needle and all Left Back sts onto needle holding Left Front. 45 sts.

LEFT HOOD
Work 6 rws in St st, ending with a WS row.
Next Row: K1, m1, k to end.
Work 11 rows in St st.
Repeat these 12 rows 5 times more.
51 sts. Hood measures 12 inches.

Row 1: K43, W&T.
Row 2: P to end.
Row 3: K35, W&T.
Row 4: P to end.
Row 5: K27, W&T.
Row 6: P to end.
Row 7: K19, W&T.
Row 8: P to end.
Row 9: K11, W&T.
Row 10: P to end.
Row 11: K all sts. When you encounter a wrapped st, pick up the wrap and place it on the left needle, then k it tog with the wrapped st.
Do not break yarn.
Join Left Hood to Right Hood along top edge using a Three-Needle Bind Off. Break yarn.

Finishing

I-CORD TRIM
Using circular needle and CC, with WS facing and beg at front corner of Left Front, pick up and p 1 st in each row up left front edge, around front edge of hood, and down right front edge. Remove crochet chain from CO end of i-cord on Right Front. Place these 4 sts on double-pointed needle and, using CC, work Applied i-cord around front edges and hood of garment. Graft live sts of i-cord just worked to held sts of i-cord on Left Front.

Using circular needle and CC, with WS facing and beg at outer edge of Right Front next to end of i-cord from CO, pick up and p 5 sts in every 4 CO sts and 1 st in each 2-row step between CO rows around outer curve of Right Front, 1 st in each row along right side edge, and 5 sts in every 4 CO sts and 1 st in each 2-row step between CO rows around outer curve of Right Back. Remove crochet chain from CO end of i-cord on Right Back. Place these 4 sts on double pointed needle and, using CC, work Applied i-cord along right side edge. Graft live sts of i-cord just worked to held sts of i-cord on Right Front.

Pick up sts and work Applied i-cord along left side edge in the same way, picking up sts beg at outer edge of Left Back next to end of i-cord, and working Applied i-cord beg at outer edge of Left Front.

Using circular needle and CC, with WS facing and beg at top back point of hood, pick up and p 1 st in each row along center back edge of left side of hood and Left Back.

Using CC, CO 4 sts and work Applied i-Cord along left center Back edge. Sew Right Back to Left Back at center edge behind Applied i-cord.

Remove crochet chain from CO end of i-cord from Left Back and graft to held sts of i-cord from Right Back.

Sew in ends. Block as desired.

TASSEL

Cut an 8-inch piece of CC yarn and lay it along the edge of a CD case.

Wrap more CC yarn snugly and evenly around the CD case several dozen times, so the 8-inch piece of yarn is inside the wraps.

Tie the 8-inch piece of yarn tightly around the wraps, so they are all held together in a small bundle.

Cut the wraps of yarn at the end opposite the tie.

Wrap another piece of CC yarn around all wraps, ¾–1 inch below the tie.

Wrap it tightly around all strands several times, then use a tapestry needle to sew both ends of this piece of yarn inside the head of the tassel. Use the 8-inch piece of yarn to sew the tassel to the point of the hood.

Abbreviations

alt	alternate	**k2tog**	knit two together
approx	approximately	**m**	meter(s)
beg	begin(ning)	**MC**	main color
bet	between	**m1**	make one by…
BO	bind off (cast off)		(lifted increase)
cab	cable	**mm**	millimeters
CC	contrasting color	**mult**	multiple
circ	circular needle	**opp**	opposite
cn	cable needle	**oz**	ounce(s)
CO	cast on	**p**	purl
cont	continue(ing)	**p2tog**	purl two together
dec	decrease(ing)	**patt(s)**	pattern(s)
div	divide	**PM**	place marker
DPN	double-pointed	**psso**	pass slipped
	needle(s)		stitch(es) over
foll	follow(s)(ing)	**rem**	remaining
g	gram(s)	**rep**	repeat
garter st	garter stitch	**rev St st**	reverse Stockinette
	(knit every row)		stitch (purl RS rows,
inc	increase(ing)		knit WS rows)
incl	include(ing)	**RS**	right side(s)
inst	instructions	**rnd(s)**	round(s)
k	knit	**sc**	single crochet
kfb	knit into front and	**SSK**	slip 2 stitches as if to
	back of stitch		knit to RH needle,
krb	knit into row below		knit 2 stitches
	to increase		together with LH
k tbl	knit through back		needle
	of loop	**SSP**	slip 2 stitches as if to
			purl, purl together
		sl	slip
		sl1-k2	Slip 1 st knitwise,
		tog-psso	k2tog, pass slipped
			st over last st, 2 sts
			decreased
		slp	slip one as if to purl
		sl st	slip stitch
		st(s)	stitch(es)
		St st	Stockinette stitch
			(knit RS rows, purl
			WS rows)
		tbl	through back of
			loop(s)
		tog	together
		WYIF	with yarn in front
		WYIF	with yarn in back
		WS	wrong side(s)
		YO	yarn over
		* *	repeat directions
			between ** as
			indicated

Techniques

Crochet/Provisional Cast On
Using waste yarn, work a crochet chain several sts longer than the number of sts to be cast on. Starting 1 or 2 sts in from end of chain and using working yarn, pick up and k 1 st in the back loop of each st until the required number of sts have been worked. Later, the chain will be unraveled and the resulting live sts picked up.

Intarsia
When working color work in Intarsia, different sections of each row are worked with different colors. For this pattern, it is necessary to use a different ball of yarn for each area of color. When switching from one color to the next, drop the color you have been knitting with, and bring the yarn for the next color up under the yarn of the previous color before you continue knitting. This will twist the two yarns around each other. It is very important to do this; if you do not wrap the yarns in this way, the areas of color will not be joined, and you will have holes in your work.

Three-Needle Bind Off
Hold both pieces of knitting with right sides together. *Insert needle into first st on front needle and first st on back needle, and knit them together. Repeat this for the next st on the front and back needles. Draw the first st worked over the second st.*
Repeat from * to * until all sts have been bound off. Break yarn and draw through remaining st.

Wrap & Turn [W&T]—aka Short Rows
Work up to the spot where you need to begin your short rows.
With the yarn in front, slip the next stitch to your R needle.
Bring the yarn to the back, passing it in front of the slipped stitch.
Slip the stitch from the R needle back to the L needle.
Turn your piece and prepare to work back in the direction you just came from.

Pick Up (and Knit)
To pick up, slip the tip of your needle through the work, wrap yarn around needle as if to knit, pull yarn through to the front to form a stitch and leave on RH needle.
To pick up and knit, pick up stitch as above, knit it and leave on RH needle before picking up next stitch.

Acknowledgments

The authors have some props to give. First and foremost, to each other. We couldn't have, wouldn't have done this book alone, no way, no how. Wanna test a friendship? Write a book together. (We passed.)

Our designers get huge thanks for their amazing designs and ceaseless patience with the book process. The fabulous Glamazons +1, our beautiful Big Girl models: Jackie, Laura, Meryl, Natalie, and Sandy—every single one of them f-ing gorgeous, gorgeous, and more gorgeous (check them out at www.glamazongirls.com).

We thank our Technical Editor, Mandy Moore, who cared about this book as much as we did. We thank Erica Mulherin, the wonder illustrator, for her speed and skill. We thank Sarah (the cake goddess), Sharyn, Lynne, Stephanie, Raina—all the girls at Quirk who kept us in line, on time, and grammatically correct. We send special thanks to Rosy Ngo and her colleagues at Potter Craft for believing in Big Girls. Bill Milne is hugged for his beautiful photography. Kristi Porter is hugged for minding our k2togs. We love Beth Casey at Lorna's Laces for going above and beyond the call of yarn. Our friends who support, encourage, and in every way enrich our lives and personal knitting insanity: Carla, Debelah, Denny, Em, Fran, Jane, Jean, Jenna, John, Julie, Karla, Latifa/Janita, Lorena, Maggie, Matt, Rob, Shannon, Stephannie, Suzanne. We thank the Manhattan and Brooklyn locations that welcomed us, our knitwear, and our cameras: Baked (www.bakednyc.com), Brooklyn General (www.brooklyn-general.com), Freebird Books (www.freebirdbooks.com), and Seaport Flowers (www.seaportflowers.com). Yarn was graciously and generously provided by the list of companies on page 157. For technical support, props to Skype, iPod, Apple Computer, Guinness, Starbucks, and Espresso Royale. Candye Kane provided the theme music, and Wendy Shanker gets our eternal thanks for divine Big Girl inspiration.

Jillian thanks her children for trying to understand about Mama & the book. Amy thanks Newton for bunny cuddles when it all got to be too much, and thanks Boeing and Squeeze for bringing up the rear—and especially Philly, for more than can be said.

Meet the Designers

Jenna Adorno's grandmother taught her to knit when she was 18. It did not turn into an obsession until she was 26 and trying, unsuccessfully, to conceive. Nine years later, her son is five years old, and both he and her partner of eleven years are still regular recipients of Jenna's knitting. She lives in Seattle and works in the software industry by day, but dreams of being paid fabulously to design knit garments full time.

Libby Baker hasn't been able to let go of her needles since her first stitch in 2001. She keeps track of all the resulting projects on her blog, Creazativity (creazativity.typepad.com) and tries to sort out the resulting yarn entanglements at her home in Englewood, Colorado.

Emma Crew lives near Seattle with her husband and son. Her primary creative obsessions are knitting and spinning. Non-fibery pursuits include co-founding the charity www.madewithlovebyaliberal.org, promoting autism education, singing with the Seattle Symphony Chorale, and spending too much time on the internet, where you can find her at www.emmacrew.com.

Kate Gilbert has been obsessed with knitting since she first taught herself at age 16. Since then, she has acquired a rather large stash, knitting and designing everything from hats to underwear and creating her blog and website at www.kategilbert.com.

Jodi Green was first taught to knit by her high school art history teacher, and quickly amassed the ugliest collection of handknitted socks ever. These days she combines her knitting with printmaking, sewing, sculpture, and drawing to create large-scale prints and installations. You can see some of this work, as well as her other knitwear designs, at her website: www.jodigreen.ca.

Alison Hansel is a philosopher, a mother, a knitter, and a blogger living in Boston. She always wanted beautiful, long legs, so she knit some. Her website is at alison.knitsmiths.us

Sivia Harding is obsessed with beads and knitting! Three years ago she started a self-published line of knitted and beaded designs available in yarn stores and from her website, www.siviaharding.com. She lives in Vancouver with her husband and cat, Mooshie, who achieved fame as the cat model on the cover of Cat Bordhi's *Second Treasury of Magical Knitting.*

Rebecca Hatcher lived in Los Angeles, where she honed her orange peeling skills, until she entered second grade. Now, she works as a library and archival consultant at a nonprofit outside Boston, where she still does not blog (although she loves reading them).

Stefanie Japel's knitwork runs the gamut from purely conceptual to absolutely wearable. Her work has been exhibited at the Baltimore Museum of Art and featured on the television program *Knitty Gritty.* Stefanie's knitwear patterns can be found in the pages of several knitting books, in the online magazines *Magknits* and *Knitty,* and on her own website, www.glampyre.com.

Michelle Katerberg lives and knits on Canada's West Coast in Vancouver, B.C. Her design philosophy is that form and function are each enhanced by the other. Michelle runs the e-mail knitting list knit2fit@googlegroups.com. You can learn more about her knitting compulsions at www.knitnaq.com. For more on her other projects, including web design, visit www.GrowAnIdea.com.

Kate Kuckro lives in San Francisco, where she spends as much time as possible knitting, crafting, and baking. When Kate was little, her grandmother Mutti taught her continental knitting with yucky acrylic yarn. She abandoned each project soon after she started. Equipped with nicer yarn and much more patience, Kate taught herself to knit again in college. She has been happily designing and knitting all sorts of things ever since. To see more of her knits and patterns, visit www.simplycrafted.com.

Joan McGowan-Michael has been in one end or another of the rag business for more than 20 years. She now happily engages in her true calling, designing romantic and vintage inspired knits that include plenty of plus-sizing. See more of her work at www.whiteliesdesigns.com. Joan has a book of vintage-inspired knitting designs coming in Spring 2006.

Jordana Paige began her knitting products company, Jordana Paige (www.jordanapaige.com), while in college pursuing a business degree with an emphasis in marketing. Inspired to create products for women who were not the stereotypical "grandma knitter," and with encouragement from her family, Jordana took a chance, and became an entrepreneur. Today Jordana lives in California where she runs her business and designs knitwear full time. She is tickled that she gets to be paid for doing what she loves.

Kristi Porter is a knitwear designer, technical editor, teacher, and author, whose work has been featured in *Knit Wit* and the *Knitgrrl* book series. She published her first book, *Knitting for Dogs,* in 2005. She is the designer for Curious Creek Fibers and has appeared on the DIY television series *Knitty Gritty.* A regular contributor of features and patterns to *Knitty,* Kristi has been involved with this online magazine since its inception. She makes her home in La Jolla, California.

Stephannie Roy has been designing handknits for about three years and her designs have appeared at *Knitty* and in *Knit Wit.* She is also a Post-Doctoral Fellow specializing in health and media studies at the University of Toronto. Read about her adventures as a thinker, knitter, mother, and opinionated woman on her blog at www.acunningplan.typepad.com.

Terri Shea discovered her fiber addiction as a girl, when she embroidered flowers on her linens using colored sewing thread. She learned to knit around 1999 and began selling designs in 2002, after the dot-com crash and the birth of her first daughter left her home with nothing to show at the end of the day but 18 dirty diapers. Terri has designed for books, *Knitter's Magazine,* Cherry Tree Hill Yarns, Plymouth Yarns, *Cast On Magazine,* and *KnitNet.com.* Her self-published patterns and blog are online at www.spinningwheel.net.

Jaya Srikrishnan is a rebel knitter. She likes to see what happens when rules are broken. Her feet are coddled in hand-knit socks for most of the year. It appears that she was born knitting because no one in her family remembers when she learned. She finds time to knit every day, despite a busy life, and is rarely seen without her knitting. She is also a geek. Her Palm OS PDA is an adjunct to her knitting and she is dysfunctional without it. Jaya is the expert for Palmsource's Expert Guide on Knitting at www.palmsource.com/interests/knitting.

Carol Sulcoski left the practice of law to become a full-time mother to three, count 'em, three kids. She learned to knit as a child but did not become obsessive about it until adulthood. She is a staff member at Rosie's Yarn Cellar in Philadelphia (www.rosiesyarncellar.com) and regularly designs for the shop. Her designs have also appeared in *Knitty* and *KnitNet.com.* She lives outside Philadelphia with her husband and kids, knitting madly whenever she isn't refilling sippy cups or picking up dry cleaning.

Amy M. Swenson lives in Calgary, Alberta, with her three cats. Since 2003, Amy has printed her own line of original patterns, IndiKnits, which can be found in yarn shops across North America. More information on her knitwear designs can be found at www.indiknits.com.

Deb White finisheded her first sweater was when she was 14, and her parents wanted to find some way to entertain her on a family trip. It was very pink and very fuzzy. Since then, she has made it her mission to clothe in knitwear her husband, her 7-year-old daughter, other family, friends, and even casual acquaintances. Deb's work has appeared in *Knitty* and in *New Knits on the Block: A Guide to Knitting What Kids Really Want* by Vicki Howell.

Shop Till You Drop

Brown Sheep
100662 County Road #16
Mitchell, NE 69357
800-826-9136
www.brownsheep.com

Cascade Yarns
1224 Andover Park East
Tukwila, WA 98188
www.cascadeyarns.com

Crystal Palace
160 23rd Street
Richmond, CA 94804
510-237-9988
www.straw.com/cpy

Dale of Norway
In Canada:
Estelle Designs
2220 Midland Avenue, Unit 65
Scarborough, ON M1P 3E6
800-387-5167
info@estelledesigns.ca

In the United States:
Dale of Norway Inc.
N16 W23390 Stoneridge Drive, Suite A
Waukesha, WI 53188
262-544-1996

Elann
In Canada:
PO Box 18125, 1215C–56th Street
Delta, BC V4L 2M4

In the United States:
PO Box 1018
Point Roberts, WA 98281-1018
604-952-4096
www.elann.com

Filatura di Crosa
In Canada:
Diamond Yarn
www.diamondyarn.com

In the United States:
Tahki Stacy Charles
www.tahkistacycharles.com

JCA
(Artful Yarns/Jo Sharp)
35 Scales Lane
Townsend, MA 01469
978-597-8794

K.F.I
(Noro Yarns)
PO Box 336
315 Bayview Avenue
Amityville, NY 11701
516-546-3600 (tel)
516-546-6871 (fax)

**Lanaknits Designs/
Hemp for Knitting**
320 Vernon Street, Suite 3B
Nelson, BC, Canada V1L 4E4
888-301-0011
www.lanaknits.com

Lorna's Laces
4229 North Honore Street
Chicago, IL 60613
773-935-3803
www.lornaslaces.net

Louet Sales
In Canada:
RR #4
Prescott, ON, Canada K0E 1T0

In the United States:
808 Commerce Park Drive
Ogdensburg, NY 13669
613-925-4502
www.louet.com

Rowan
Westminster Fibers Inc.
4 Townsend West, Unit 8
Nashua, NH 03063
603-886-5041
info@westminsterfibers.com

S. R. Kertzer Limited
50 Trowers Road
Woodbridge, ON, Canada L4L 7K6
800-263-2354
www.kertzer.com

Tahki Stacy Charles
(Filatura di Crosa, Tahki)
8000 Cooper Ave, Building #1
Glendale, NY 11385
800-338-YARN
www.tahkistacycharles.com

Unique Kolours
(Colinette Yarns)
28 N. Bacton Hill Road
Malvern, PA 19355
800-25-2DYE4

White Lies Designs
PO Box 214883
Sacramento, CA 95821
916-450-8160
www.whiteliesdesigns.com

NOTIONS
Earthenwood Studio Buttons
(page 60)
www.earthenwood.net

Ghee's Bag Frame and Feet
(page 132)
2620 Centenary Boulevard, 2–250
Shreveport, LA 71104
318-226-1701
www.ghees.com

Essential Reads for Big Girls

FASHION AND LIFESTYLE BOOKS

Bernall, Bonnie. *Bountiful Women: Large Women's Secrets for Living the Life They Desire.* Wildcat Canyon Press, 2000.

Brin, Geri and Tish Jett. *Figure It Out: The Real Woman's Guide to Great Style.* Sixth and Spring Books, 2004.

Emme, et al. *True Beauty: Positive Attitudes and Practical Tips from the World's Leading Plus-Size Model.* Berkley Publishing, 1996.

Farro, Rita. *Life Is Not a Dress Size.* Chilton Book Company, 1996.

Feldon, Leah. *Does This Make Me Look Fat? The Definitive Rules for Dressing Thin for Every Height, Size, and Shape.* Villard, 2000.

Lippincott, Catherine. *Well Rounded: Eight Simple Steps for Changing Your Life…Not Your Size.* Pocket Books, 1997.

Manheim, Camryn. *Wake Up, I'm Fat!* Broadway Books, 1999.

Nanfeldt, Suzan. *Plus Style: The Plus-Size Guide to Looking Great.* Plume, 1996.

Saboura, Sam. *Sam Saboura's Real Style: Style Secrets for Real Women with Real Bodies.* Clarkson Potter, 2005.

Shanker, Wendy. *The Fat Girl's Guide to Life.* Bloomsbury, 2004.

Wann, Marilyn. *Fat!So?* Ten Speed Press, 1998.

Weston, Michelle. *Learning Curves: Living Your Life in Full and with Style.* Crown Publishers, 2001.

Woodall, Trinny and Susannah Constantine. *What Not to Wear.* Riverhead Books, 2002.

KNITTING BOOKS

Allen, Pam. *Knitting for Dummies.* Wiley Publishing, 2002.

Buss, Katharina. *Big Book of Knitting.* Sterling Publications, 1999.

Duncan, Ida Riley. *Knit to Fit: A Comprehensive Guide to Hand and Machine Knitting.* Liveright Publishing, 1966.

Ellen, Alison. *Hand Knitting: New Directions.* The Crowood Press, 2002.

Hiatt, June. *The Principles of Knitting.* Vogue Knitting, Butterick Company, 1989.

New, Debbie. *Unexpected Knitting.* Schoolhouse Press, 2003.

Newton, Deborah. *Designing Knitwear.* Taunton Press, 1992.

Michelson, Carmen and Mary-Ann Davis. *The Knitter's Guide to Sweater Design.* Interweave Press, 1989.

Righetti, Maggie. *Knitting in Plain English.* St. Martin's Press, 1986.

Righetti, Maggie. *Sweater Design in Plain English.* St. Martin's Press, 1990.

Stanley, Montse. *Creating & Knitting Your Own Designs for a Perfect Fit.* Harper & Row, 1982.

Stanley, Montse. *Knitter's Handbook.* Reader's Digest, 1993.

Whiting, Maggie. *The Progressive Knitter.* BT Batsford LTD, 1988.

Zilboorg, Anna. *Knitting for Anarchists.* Feet on the Ground Press, 2002.

SEWING BOOKS

Not a lot has been written about sewing specifically for Big Girls. However, we found loads of useful information in these sewing books.

Betzina, Sandra. *Fast Fit: Easy Pattern Alterations for Every Figure.* The Taunton Press, 2003.

Deckert, Barbara. *Sewing for Plus Sizes.* The Taunton Press, 2002.

Grigg Hazen, Gale. *Fantastic Fit for Every Body.* Rodale Press, 1998.

Palmer, Cherie. *The Perfect Fit.* Charles Scribner's Sons, 1975.

Zapp, Anna. *The Zapp Method of Couture Sewing.* Krause Publications, 2004.

MAGAZINE ARTICLES

McGowan-Michael, Joan. "Size Matters: Knitting for the Amply Blessed Woman," *Cast On Magazine,* Winter/Spring 2002.

Veronik, Avery. "Short Rows: A Few Stitches Short of a Row," *Interweave Knits,* Winter 2004.

WEB SITES

Knitty Magazine @ knitty.com

Big Girl Knits online @ biggirlknits.com

Index

Italic page numbers refer to illustrations.